English Language Learners With Special Education Needs

Identification, Assessment, and Instruction

1-10	Ch. 1
1-31	Ch 2
2-4	ch. 3/4
2-14	ch. 5
3-7	6, 7, 8
3-14	9

2-28 ref. 4

Printed in the United States of America
10 9 8 7 6 5 4 3 2

Professional Practice Series 2

Editorial/production supervision: Joy Kreeft Peyton and Donald A. Ranard
Copyediting/proofreading: Amy Fitch
Design and cover: SAGARTdesign

ISBN 1-887744-69-X

Prepared for publication by the ERIC Clearinghouse on Languages and Linguistics. Published by the Center for Applied Linguistics and Delta Systems Co., Inc.

The writing and production of this volume were supported by the U.S. Department of Education, Office of Educational Research and Improvement, National Library of Education, under Contract No. ED-99-CO-0008. The opinions expressed in this publication do not necessarily reflect the positions or policies of the U.S. Department of Education.

Library of Congress Cataloging-in-Publication Data

English language learners with special education needs : Identification, assessment, and instruction / Alfredo J. Artiles, Alba A. Ortiz, editors.
     p. cm. — (Professional practice series ; 2)
  Includes biliograpical references.
  ISBN 1-887744-69-X (alk. paper)
    1. English language—Study and teaching—Foreign speakers. 2. Learning disabled—Education. 3. Individualized instruction. 4. Learning disabilities. 5. Special education. I. Artiles, Alfredo J. II. Ortiz, Alba A. III. Professional practice series 2 (Center for Applied Linguistics).

PE1128.A2 E488 2002
428'0071—dc21

                  2002073738

English Language Learners With Special Education Needs

Identification, Assessment, and Instruction

Alfredo J. Artiles
Alba A. Ortiz

Editors

In memory of our friend and colleague Candy Bos,
for her legacy of innovative and socially significant scholarship
in the field of special education

Contents

viii   The Professional Practice Series

x   Acknowledgments

Introduction

3   **CHAPTER 1**

English Language Learners With Special Education Needs:
Contexts and Possibilities
Alfredo J. Artiles and Alba A. Ortiz

Prevention and Early Intervention

31   **CHAPTER 2**

Prevention of School Failure and Early Intervention for
English Language Learners
Alba A. Ortiz

Assessment and Identification

51   **CHAPTER 3**

Toward a New Model of Assessment
Richard A. Figueroa

65   **CHAPTER 4**

Considerations in the Assessment of English Language
Learners Referred to Special Education
Alba A. Ortiz and James R. Yates

87   **CHAPTER 5**

Parent-Professional Collaboration in Culturally Sensitive
Assessment
Shernaz B. García

Instruction

107 **CHAPTER 6**
Culturally and Linguistically Responsive Instructional Planning
Nancy Cloud

133 **CHAPTER 7**
Effective Pedagogy for English Language Learners in Inclusive
Classrooms
Lorri Johnson Santamaría, Todd V. Fletcher, and Candace S. Bos

159 **CHAPTER 8**
Walking the Talk: The Joys and Challenges of Critical
Pedagogy
Barbara S. C. Goldstein

Conclusion

191 **CHAPTER 9**
Educating English Language Learners With Special Education
Needs: Trends and Future Directions
Leonard M. Baca

203 **References**

245 **About the Contributors**

The Professional Practice Series

Like almost everyone else in today's fast-paced world, teachers and education administrators are very busy people. In addition to working with students in the classroom and designing and overseeing educational programs, they are likely to be involved in curriculum development; design and development of instructional materials; committee assignments; coordination of after-school activities; and communication with parents, counselors, community leaders, and others involved in the education of their students. In addition, they need to stay abreast of new research and developments in their subject areas and in the field of education. Reading the literature, attending conferences, and participating in and leading workshops and in-service training sessions are all part of their ongoing professional development.

Teachers and administrators need ready access to clear and reliable information about effective practices in language education. The *Professional Practice Series*, developed by the ERIC Clearinghouse on Languages and Linguistics and published by the Center for Applied Linguistics and Delta Systems, is designed to provide practitioners with current information on topics, trends, and techniques in language teaching. Each volume begins with an overview of the topic and the chapters in the book. Each chapter focuses on a particular aspect of the topic and the knowlege we have about it. The chapters describe the strategies and techniques used by effective teachers and administrators and offer practical guidelines and suggestions to help others implement similar strategies in their own classrooms, schools, and districts. Each volume closes with a summary of key points in the book and general guidelines and recommendations.

It is our hope that the *Professional Practice Series* will provide language educators with accessible, timely information, supported by theory and research, that will help them improve or enhance their teaching and their programs.

Jeanne Rennie and Joy Kreeft Peyton, Series Editors
Center for Applied Linguistics
Washington, DC

For online information about this series and other books included in it, visit www.practiceseries.com.

Acknowledgments

This book describes the complex challenges involved in serving English language learners with special education needs. The authors belong to a small group of educators in this country who have focused their research and teaching on this population of learners. We thank them for their willingness to share their knowledge and for providing the field with expert guidance in designing effective early intervention, assessment, and instructional programs and services for these students.

Thanks also to Joy Peyton at the Center for Applied Linguistics (CAL) for recognizing the critical need for this book, for overseeing the project, and for her sage editorial advice. We are particularly grateful to Don Ranard, a consulting editor at CAL, for his insightful comments and excellent editorial suggestions. Joy and Don ensured that we were always clear, concise, and coherent.

Initial drafts of this book were reviewed by Else Hamayan, Illinois Resource Center in Des Plaines, Illinois, and Robert Rueda, University of Southern California. We thank them for their thoughtful and helpful comments.

We also wish to thank Amy Fitch for her editorial assistance and Vincent Sagart (SAGARTdesign) for his design and layout of the book.

Finally, we are grateful to Lynn Spencer, the U.S. Department of Education's Contracting Officer's Representative for ERIC/CLL, for her helpful comments during the preparation of this book.

Alfredo J. Artiles, Associate Professor
Special Education
Vanderbilt University, Nashville, Tennessee

Alba A. Ortiz, Professor
Special Education
President's Chair for Education Academic Excellence
The University of Texas at Austin

Introduction

English Language Learners With Special Education Needs: Contexts and Possibilities

Alfredo J. Artiles, *Vanderbilt University*
Alba A. Ortiz, *University of Texas at Austin*

The Individuals With Disabilities Education Act Amendments (1997) drew attention to a continuing problem in American schools: the dis proportionate number of learners from culturally and linguistically diverse backgrounds in special education programs. Research findings (Donovan & Cross, 2002; Artiles, Trent, & Palmer, in press; Individuals With Disabilities Education Act Amendments, 1997) indicate that some racial and ethnic groups had disabilities in greater numbers than would be expected, given their percentage in the general student population, while other groups were significantly underrepresented.[1] For example,

---

[1]The historic pattern has been overrepresentation in the so-called *high-incidence disabilities*, which include mental retardation, learning disabilities, and emotional/behavioral disorders. The term *mental retardation* is defined as "substantial limitations in present functioning. It is characterized by significantly subaverage intellectual functioning . . . with related limitations in two or more of the following . . . skill areas: communication, self-care, home living, social skills, community use, self-direction, health and safety, functional academics, leisure, and work" (Smith, 2001, p. 230). The term *learning disability* refers to "a disorder in one or more of the basic psychological processes involved in understanding or in using language, spoken or written, that may manifest itself in an imperfect ability to listen, think, speak, read, write, spell, or do mathematical calculations, including conditions [such] as perceptual disabilities, brain injury, minimal brain dysfunction, dyslexia, and developmental aphasia. The term does not include learning problems that are primarily the result of visual, hearing, motor disabilities, mental retardation, emotional disturbance, or environmental, cultural, or economic disadvantages" (p. 128). The term *emotional disturbance* refers to

African Americans represented 16% of elementary and secondary school enrollments but 21% of students in special education; they were also more than twice as likely as their White peers to be labeled as mentally retarded (Individuals with Disabilities Education Act Amendments, 1997). On the other hand, Asian American students were underrepresented in every disability category. Congress found that English language learners posed particularly complex challenges relating to referral, assessment, and instruction, and that the services provided to these students did not effectively meet their needs.

Overrepresentation of minority students in special education is a longstanding issue. In 1968, Dunn noted that 60% to 80% of students in special education were children of color. A few years later, Mercer (1973) reported that in California, African Americans were three times and Mexican Americans four times as likely as White students to be labeled mentally retarded. Laws designed to protect the rights of learners from culturally and linguistically diverse backgrounds have failed to resolve this problem. A contributing factor is that educators and policymakers have essentially ignored the increasing diversity of America's classrooms as they have implemented reforms to raise educational standards and improve schools (Ortiz, 2000). English language learners, in particular, have been neglected in analyses of minority overrepresentation and school system reforms (Artiles, Rueda, Salazar, & Higareda, 2000).

This book explores these issues and challenges and offers recommendations for improving the general education and special education services provided to English language learners with disabilities. The chapters in this volume report recent developments in the education of English language learners with special needs and are based on alternative visions of learning, assessment, and instruction. Such alternative

---

"a condition exhibiting one or more of the following characteristics ... that adversely affects a child's educational performance: an ability to learn that cannot be explained by intellectual, sensory, or health factors; an inability to build or maintain satisfactory interpersonal relationships with peers and teachers; inappropriate types of behavior or feelings under normal circumstances; a general pervasive mood of unhappiness or depression; a tendency to develop physical symptoms of fears associated with personal or school problems" (p. 324). The same racial and ethnic minorities that are overrepresented in special education are underrepresented in programs for gifted and talented students.

assumptions view cultural and linguistic differences as resources upon which to capitalize. The book is based on the premise that the educational needs of English language learners are many and complex; thus, general, bilingual, and special educators must work together to ensure that schools address the educational needs of this population in a culturally and linguistically sensitive fashion.

In this chapter, we outline the context in which the education of English language learners with special needs is taking place. We begin with an overview of demographic changes at the national level. We then discuss the educational performance of students from culturally and linguistically diverse backgrounds and summarize disability prevalence data by race and language status. In addition, we discuss the legal and educational issues that relate to English language learners with special needs. We conclude with a brief summary of the chapters in this volume.

The Demographic Context

The 2000 Census showed that 281 million people resided in the United States, an increase of 13% from 1990 (Grieco & Cassidy, 2001). Almost 40% of U.S. citizens were members of racial and ethnic minorities. Of these, approximately 35 million, or 13%, were Latino/a, 12% African American, 4% Asian American, 1% American Indian or Alaska Native, and 8% were other racial/ethnic minority groups. These figures would be even higher if individuals who reported membership in more than one ethnic or racial group had been counted in each category.

These demographic shifts are expected to continue as the result of both birth rates and immigration trends. Birth rates are especially high among some immigrant groups. For example, Latina women during their child-bearing years have a fertility rate of 84 births per 1,000 women (Bachus & O'Connell, 1998), compared with rates of 62 and 57 per 1,000 for African American and White women respectively.

Immigration Trends

Immigration trends also contribute significantly to demographic shifts. In 2000, the foreign-born population in the United States exceeded 30 million, more than 10% of the population (U.S. Census Bureau, n.d.). Of these, more than half are Latino/a, more than 25% are Asian and Pacific Islanders, and about 6% are from Africa and Oceania. The United States is also home to nearly 2,500,000 refugees from Africa, Asia, Central and South America, and the Middle East (U.S. Department of State, Bureau of Population, Refugees, and Migration, 2002).

The country's demographic changes are reflected in public school enrollments. In 1998, almost 40% of the nearly 47,000,000 public school students in Grades 1 through 12 had culturally and linguistically diverse home backgrounds (National Center for Educational Statistics, 2000). Almost 10 million came from homes where languages other than English were spoken. The language minority population is growing at a significantly faster rate than is the overall student population (National Clearinghouse for Bilingual Education, 1995) and will soon outnumber the English-speaking student population in more than 50 major U.S. cities (Teachers of English to Speakers of Other Languages, 1997).

English Language Learners

More than 400 languages are spoken by English language learners nationwide (Kindler, 2002). Spanish speakers make up approximately 75% of the language minority population, while speakers of Arabic, Cambodian, Cantonese, Creole, French, Hmong, Korean, Lao, Navajo, Russian, Tagalog, and Vietnamese each represent from 1 to 4%. English language learners also vary widely in their background experiences and in their relationship to the mainstream culture and language: Some are children of recent immigrants; others migrated to the United States at an early age; and still others were born here in ethnic communities where the social, cultural, and linguistics norms are distinct from those of the mainstream culture (Fillmore, 1991).

In 1996 and 1997, state education agencies reported serving 3,452,073 English language learners in public and nonpublic schools, an increase of almost 7% from figures reported in 1995 and 1996 (Macías, 1998). Almost 50% of the nation's public schools reported that they enrolled at least one English language learner (Han, Baker, & Rodriguez, 1997). While available data show dramatic increases in this population, the number is likely to be an underestimate because of the great variation in definitions and criteria used to identify students who are eligible for special language support. For example, the U.S. Census Bureau estimates the prevalence of limited English proficiency based on responses given to questions about the languages used in the home and the household members' ability to speak English (Hopstock & Bucaro, 1993). Schools, on the other hand, typically use oral language assessments and measures of English academic achievement, along with grades and teacher recommendations, to identify English language learners. In some states, students are considered limited English proficient if they score in the "less than fluent" range on an oral language test. In others, they qualify for services if they score below district standards on English reading and writing assessments (Hopstock & Bucaro, 1993). Prevalence estimates are also affected by economic, legal, and political forces, such as the high mobility of English language learners and their immigration status.

Educational Performance of Learners From Culturally Diverse Backgrounds

Substantial evidence indicates that educational services offered to students with culturally and linguistically diverse home backgrounds are not sufficient to meet their needs. Latino/a and African American students are less likely than their White counterparts to complete high school or to demonstrate competency in reading, writing, mathematics, history, geography, and science (Durán, 1983; National Center for Educational Statistics, 1999). Across grades, no more than 12% of African American students and 18% of Latino/a students met proficiency standards in these subjects as compared with a 40% rate for White students (National Education Goals Panel, 1995). In 1995, the grade retention rates were almost 19% for African Americans and 15% for Latino/a but 2.1% for White students. Overall, the 1997 high school dropout rate was 11% for 16- to 24-year-olds. It was 25% for Latino/a students in this age group and 39% for those who were foreign born (National Center for Educational Statistics, 1999).

In 1996 to 1997, the grade retention rates for English language learners ranged from 0.7% to 100% across states, while dropout rates ranged from a low of 0.3% to a high of 6.8% (Macías, 1998). Some of these rates may be even higher; some states, including California and Texas, did not report these data. Students who drop out of school have the highest rate of children born out of wedlock, lower lifetime incomes, and a greater incidence of other societal problems that negatively affect the nation's economy (National Governors' Association, 1987; Singh, 1986). The primary reason for leaving school is a lack of academic success. Lack of academic success is also the major reason for referral of English language learners to special education (Ortiz et al., 1985).

English Language Learners in Special Education

Placement rates in special education for racial and ethnic minorities vary greatly across the nation (Artiles & Zamora-Durán, 1997; Ortiz & Yates, 1983; Rice, 1995; Robertson, Kushner, Starks, & Drescher, 1994). Data gathered by Henderson, Abbot, and Strang (1993) illustrated similar national disparities for English language learners. According to these data, 26.5% of English language learners in Massachusetts, 25.3% in South Dakota, and 20.1% in New Mexico were in special education programs, while less than 1% of this population of learners in Colorado, Maryland, and North Carolina were placed in such programs. In Texas, English language learners were up to five times as likely to be receiving special education support in one district as in another (Robertson, Kushner, Starks, & Drescher, 1994).

As with trends reported in the 1980s (Finn, 1982), overrepresentation in special education appears to be associated with the size of the

English language learner population in school districts and the availability of language support programs. Artiles, Rueda, et al. (2000) analyzed the 1998-1999 special education placement data for English language learners in several large school districts in southern California with a student enrollment of more than 500,000 and found that English language learners were overrepresented at the state and district levels.

Grade level and limited proficiency in either the native language or English were also associated with overrepresentation in these districts. English language learners in secondary grades and those with limited language proficiency in the first and second language were the most overrepresented in programs for students with mental retardation, learning disabilities, and language and speech impairments.[2] English language learners in secondary grades received less language support than did their counterparts in elementary grades. Artiles, Rueda, et al. (2000) also found that English language learners were more likely than English speakers to be placed in high incidence disability categories. Moreover, those receiving the least language support were more likely to be placed in special education programs; for instance, learners receiving all of their instruction in English were almost three times as likely to be in special education resource rooms as those receiving some native language support. Rueda, Artiles, Salazar, and Higareda (in press) examined special education placement rates for Latino English language learners in a 5-year period (1993/94 to 1998/99) and found that the placement rate for these learners increased by 345% even though their overall representation in the district increased by only 12% within the same time period.

These data suggest the need to examine more systematically how political initiatives, availability of alternative services, and special education placement practices for English language learners interact.

---

[2] These districts distinguished between English language learners with limited proficiency in their first language and those with limited proficiency in both their first and second language.

Legislative and Legal Context for English Language Learners With Disabilities

Existing policy, law, and judicial decisions are designed to ensure that English language learners with disabilities receive an appropriate education. Overrepresentation in special education, however, suggests that these safeguards are not familiar to educators, have not been effectively implemented, or are being ignored. While it is beyond the scope of this chapter to provide a comprehensive review of the legal issues relating to English language learners with disabilities, some of the most relevant laws and legal cases are highlighted here. They are presented chronologically because legislation and litigation typically incorporate or expand the rights and legal precedents established by earlier laws and court rulings.

Civil Rights Act

The Civil Rights Act (1964), and its subsequent judicial interpretations, prohibits federally funded programs from discriminating in their services on the basis of race, color, religion, sex, or national origin. According to the act, federally funded programs cannot offer services to an individual that are different from, not equal to, or not as effective as those offered to other individuals; provide separate aid, benefits, or services to an individual or group unless it can be shown that it is necessary to do so to ensure that services are effective; and limit an individual's enjoyment of any right, privilege, advantage, or opportunity afforded others (U.S. Commission on Civil Rights, 1997).

On May 25, 1970, the U.S. Department of Health, Education, and Welfare (HEW) issued a memorandum explaining that it is a violation of the Civil Rights Act to exclude children from effective participation in school because they cannot understand or speak English. The memorandum required that school districts take steps to rectify children's language "deficiencies"; avoid labeling students as mentally retarded based on criteria that reflected their English proficiency; ensure that ability groupings or tracking systems designed to meet the language needs of students were not "dead ends"; and notify minority parents of school activities, providing native language support when necessary (Lyons, 1992).

Bilingual Education Act

The Bilingual Education Act (1968), and its subsequent amendments, provided federal funding to local school districts for innovative programs for students with limited English skills. While the 1968 act did not require native language instruction, most federally funded programs initially provided it (August & Hakuta, 1997). The 1988 amendments to the act increased funding for "special alternative" programs in which only English is used and imposed a 3-year limit on participation in most bilingual education programs (Stewner-Manzanares, 1988). New provisions in 1994 reinforced the need for professional development for special language program personnel, increased attention to language maintenance and foreign language instruction, and augmented support for research and evaluation (Title VII of the Improving America's School Act of 1994).

Diana v. State Board of Education

Plaintiffs in *Diana v. State Board of Education* (1970), filed on behalf of Mexican American children in Monterey County, California, alleged that the school system was inaccurately identifying Spanish-speaking children as mentally retarded on the basis of IQ tests administered in English. In a preliminary settlement, the judge ordered that all Mexican American children who previously had been placed in special education be reassessed in their first language and in English, or by using nonverbal IQ tests (Valdés & Figueroa, 1994). The judge also mandated that an IQ test appropriate for Mexican American students be developed and called for the monitoring of school districts to identify racial and ethnic disparities in special education placements.

Vocational Rehabilitation Act

The Vocational Rehabilitation Act (1973) is the civil rights law that protects individuals with disabilities. The act states that no otherwise-qualified individual with a disability can be excluded from, or denied the benefits of, programs or activities supported with federal funds.

Together, the Vocational Rehabilitation Act and the Civil Rights Act are the bases for the protection of the rights of individuals who are limited

English proficient and have disabilities. English language learners have a right to participate in both bilingual education and special education programs (Baca, 1998). Denying access to these programs violates both the Civil Rights Act, which prohibits services that are different from, not equal to, or not as effective as those provided to other individuals, and the Vocational Rehabilitation Act, which prohibits the denial of programs and services to individuals with disabilities who would otherwise be eligible for such services. According to Baca (1998), "Just because a bilingual exceptional child qualifies for services under special education does not mean that he/she is automatically disqualified for services under bilingual education or vice versa" (p. 93). English language learners need and have the right to an individually designed bilingual program of special instruction that builds on the home language and culture (Baca & de Valenzuela, 1998).

Lau v. Nichols

In the 1974 case, *Lau v. Nichols,* the Supreme Court ruled that the San Francisco Unified School District violated Title VI of the Civil Rights Act when it failed to provide services to help Chinese-speaking students learn English. While the Court did not require that students be provided bilingual instruction, the Department of Health, Education, and Welfare subsequently issued remedies requiring that schools offer bilingual, multilingual, or transitional bilingual education for eligible participants (August & Hakuta, 1997).

Larry P. v. Riles

In the 1979 case, *Larry P. v. Riles,* the judge ordered an injunction against the use of IQ tests that did not take into account the cultural backgrounds and experiences of African American children. The injunction also prohibited the placement of African American pupils in classes for students with mental retardation based on IQ tests that had not been approved by the court (Valdés & Figueroa, 1994). Court approval could be granted to tests that were shown to be free of racial or cultural bias, that were validated for the specific purpose of identifying students with mental retardation, and that did not contribute to overrepresentation of minority students in special education. As in the *Diana* case, the state was ordered to reevaluate students in programs for the mentally retarded and to monitor racial and ethnic disparities in special education placements. The *Larry P.* case established the legal precedent that tests used with minority children must have been validated for use with that population (Valdés & Figueroa, 1994). Because *Larry P.* offered essentially the same protections to African American students as those afforded Mexican Americans in the *Diana* judgment, it provides the legal precedent against cultural bias in testing.

Court Cases Supporting Bilingual Education

Baca (1990) cites three court cases as the most significant in the development of bilingual special education services for English language learners. These are *Jose P. v. Ambach* (1983), *United Cerebral Palsy (UCP) of New York v. Board of Education of the City of New York* (1979), and *Dyrcia S. et al. v. Board of Education of the City of New York* (1979). Together, these cases require that school systems (a) use bilingual resources to identify English language learners that need special education, (b) provide evaluations that are in two languages and are nondiscriminatory, (c) provide bilingual alternatives at each stage of the special education placement process, (d) protect the rights of parents and students and develop a Spanish language version of the parents' rights booklet, and (e) hire community workers to facilitate the involvement of parents in the assessment process and in the development of their children's individualized educational plan (IEP) (Baca, 1990).

Individuals With Disabilities Education Act

Originally enacted in 1975 as the Education for all Handicapped Children, and renamed the Individuals With Disabilities Education Act in 1990, this law includes important safeguards for English language learners. The 1997 amendments to the act clearly state that students are not eligible for services if their learning problems are primarily the result of environmental, cultural, or economic disadvantage. Evaluation and placement procedures must be nondiscriminatory, and they must be conducted in the child's native language, unless it is clearly not feasible to do so. Moreover, assessment results must be considered by individuals knowledgeable about the child, about assessment, and about placement alternatives (U.S. Commission on Civil Rights, 1997). The act also requires that steps be taken to ensure that parents understand the proceedings of IEP meetings. They should know, for example, that parents with limited English have a right to an interpreter. The multidisciplinary team—the group of educators who determine a student's eligibility for special education services—must consider the language needs of English language learners when developing, reviewing, or revising IEPs. This means that IEPs should specify which instructional goals and objectives will be delivered in the native language and which will be delivered in English, using approaches appropriate for English language learners (Yates & Ortiz, 1998a).

In summary, the legislation and litigation described above serve to protect the rights of English language learners and to ensure that they are provided a free, appropriate public education (FAPE). To this end, schools need to put into place the following practices (Ortiz & Yates, 2001):

- Prevention and early intervention services to avert unnecessary special education referrals
- Referral processes that distinguish struggling learners from students who are likely to have disabilities
- Assessments conducted by qualified bilingual evaluators who (a) use instruments and procedures appropriate for English language learners; (b) provide accurate data about native language and English language performance; (c) identify modifications of instruction, methods, and materials needed for both native language and English as a second language instruction; and (d) provide data to rule out such factors as limited English proficiency, cultural differences, economic status, and opportunity to learn as the causes of learning problems
- Multidisciplinary teams made up of experts in the education of English language learners and in assessment and placement alternatives; interpreters for non-English-speaking parents, and administrators to ensure that needed bilingual special education programs and services are provided

- IEPs that are culturally and linguistically relevant and that describe the extent to which students will participate in bilingual education, English as a second language (ESL), and general education programs and in state or district accountability systems
- A variety of bilingual special education alternatives, such as special education classes that provide native language and ESL instruction and inclusive general education classes in which bilingual educators are supported by special education consultants with expertise in teaching English language learners with disabilities
- Annual reviews to ensure that language- and disability-related needs are being met and that students are progressing as expected

Educational Issues

To improve educational programs and services for English language learners with disabilities, educators need to overcome barriers embedded in the bilingual and special education fields and in current educational reform movements. They also need to improve links among different programs serving English language learners with special educational needs.

Bilingual Education

Since the inception of bilingual education, there has been a contentious debate over whether English language learners should receive native language instruction, and if so, how much and for how long (Kushner & Ortiz, 2000). There have also been numerous attempts over the years to limit programs and resources for these students by eliminating bilingual education and by making English the official language of government, education, and the workplace. (California and Arizona have abolished bilingual education, and other states are debating whether to adopt such an initiative.) Increasingly, students are expected to assimilate and conform to the mainstream culture and language (i.e., the English language used by the White middle class) as quickly as possible.

The debate about bilingual education is complicated by a general lack of understanding about second language acquisition, the crucial role that a child's native language plays in intellectual and cognitive development, and the critical relationship between native language and English language proficiency (Kushner & Ortiz, 2000). A common misconception is that English language learners are likely to experience difficulty in mastering skills in their native language and that they should therefore be taught only in English to avoid confusing them (August & Hakuta, 1997; Ortiz, 1984). Yet the literature on second language acquisition and bilingual education does not support such reasoning. Rather, it indicates that unless children with disabilities develop native language competence, they will have problems learning a second language and will experience difficulty with cognitive development as well (Cummins, 1984).

Special Education

Special education continues to be based on a model of disability (Rueda et al., in press) that locates the problem or "disease" in the child and then attempts to "cure" the problem with a series of "treatments" or interventions. Yet teachers evaluate student competence on the basis of factors other than ability; these include race, sex, economic status, language, and culture (Rueda et al., in press). The lack of appropriate assessment instruments and personnel qualified to assess English language learners (Ortiz et al., 1985; Ortiz, García, Wheeler & Maldonado-Colón, 1986) exacerbates the problem of inappropriate referrals. Consequently, the data used for special education decisions cannot distinguish disabilities from linguistic and cultural differences.

Some educators argue that if English language learners are failing in general education classes, there is no harm in placing them in special education, where they can get individualized instruction from teachers trained to remediate learning problems. Yet there is evidence to the contrary. Wilkinson and Ortiz (1986) found that after 3 years of special education intervention, Spanish-speaking students with learning disabilities actually lost ground. Their verbal and full-scale IQ scores were lower than they had been at initial placement, and their achievement scores were at essentially the same level as at entry. Neither general education nor special education programs adequately served the needs of these students.

Education Reforms

In the current climate of education reform, educators working with English language learners with special education needs have had to press for the participation of these students in reform efforts. Two of these reforms are the inclusion and the standards movements.

The inclusion movement is based on two premises; one involves rights and the other involves efficacy. Inclusion advocates contend that students with disabilities have the right to be educated with nondisabled peers. This moral argument is supported by evidence that students with disabilities do not show significant academic gains when educated in segregated special education programs (Dyson, 1999). Furthermore, researchers have shown that instructional practices in segregated and inclusive education programs do not vary significantly (Dyson, 1999).

Despite resistance to inclusion from various sectors of the education field, we have witnessed a gradual move toward more inclusive education models. Currently, more than 90% of students with disabilities are educated in the same schools that nondisabled students attend. It should be noted, however, that the inclusive education movement is not concerned only with placement in regular education contexts. Ultimately, it is interested in the promotion of academic learning, social competence, social skills, changes in societal attitudes toward those with special education needs, and positive peer relations among students of different academic abilities (Lipsky & Gartner, 1999).

Inclusive education is grounded in a set of beliefs and practices. Schools that practice inclusive education believe that all children can learn. To this end, they implement school-wide efforts to educate students with special education needs, adapt the curricula and instructional strategies to the needs of students with learning difficulties, encourage collaboration among teachers, foster a sense of community, and pay attention to standards and outcomes (Lipsky & Gartner, 1999). Despite recent efforts to develop and assess inclusive education (U.S. Department of Education, 1999), the movement has been noticeably silent about the plight of minority students in general and English language learners in particular, who happen to be overrepresented in special education programs (Artiles, 2000). In fact, emergent evidence suggests that minority students are more likely to be placed in segregated settings and less likely to benefit from special education programs than their White counterparts (Rueda et al., in press).

Another major issue facing educators is how to include English language learners and students with disabilities in standards-based reforms (Ortiz, 2000). The 1997 amendments to the Individuals With Disabilities Act emphasized that special education can be made more effective by raising expectations for students with disabilities, by giving learners access to the general education curriculum, and by making school-wide improvements that reduce the need to label children in order to address their learning needs (McLaughlin, Artiles, & Pullin, 2001; McLaughlin, Nolet, Rhim, & Henderson, 1999; Ortiz, this volume). However, students cannot meet high academic standards unless they receive high-quality instruction. Because of the severe shortage of bilingual education and special education teachers, English language learners with disabilities are often taught by the least experienced and least qualified teachers (August & Hakuta, 1997). When accountability systems involve high-stakes testing (e.g., tests used to determine whether students will be promoted or retained in grade, to rate teacher effectiveness, and to classify schools as high or low performing), English language learners are either routinely excluded because of fears that they will depress test scores, or they are referred to special education because a disability label makes it easier to justify their exclusion. Exclusion policies can have far-reaching, negative consequences for learners, not the least of which is that no one can really be held accountable for the achievement of excluded students.

Linking Instructional Programs

The education of language minority students in general, and of English language learners with disabilities in particular, is a complex task that includes ESL and bilingual education, general education, and special education programs. Bilingual education teachers must provide native language and ESL instruction. ESL teachers must help students acquire effective English skills. To do so, they must have the support of general education teachers, who in turn must use ESL strategies so that instruction is understandable to English language learners. All teachers must be able to adapt instruction for struggling learners in order to reduce grade retention rates and inappropriate referrals to special education. When students are referred, school psychologists, speech pathologists, and other assessment personnel must select instruments and procedures to ensure accurate diagnoses of disabilities, a goal that cannot be met if they rely solely on standardized tests normed on monolingual, middle-class White students or even standardized tests normed on bilingual populations. If students qualify for special education, all teachers, not only special educators, must have the skills to implement programs that simultaneously address students' language- and disability-related needs.

Overview of This Volume

This book argues that English language learners with special needs require an array of educational services that take into account their linguistic and cultural backgrounds. We argue that this dual emphasis on language and culture and on a comprehensive system of services—from pre-referral to instruction—will force professionals to transcend what until now has been the field's almost exclusive focus on student deficits.

Throughout the book, we use two terms to refer to culturally diverse student groups. *Culturally and linguistically diverse* is the broadest term and encompasses students, from African Americans to recently arrived immigrants, whose language and cultural backgrounds vary from that of the mainstream. *English language learners* are students whose first or home language is other than English and whose English skills are so limited that they cannot profit from instruction provided entirely in English without support. Increasingly, educators use the term *English language learner* in place of *limited English proficient* to avoid the negative connotation of *limited* as a descriptor of student abilities, and we have generally followed that practice in this book. However, because *limited English proficient* is still the official designation in government and in law, we use it when referring to public policy, law, or a publication that uses the term.

While information in this book will be useful to practitioners working with all culturally and linguistically diverse student groups, our primary concern is with the education of English language learners with disabilities. The book explores this topic in four sections. The first three sections—Prevention and Early Intervention, Assessment and Identification, and Instruction—discuss the continuum of services that students with special needs require. The final section—Trends and Future Directions—summarizes the most important issues raised in the previous three sections.

We now turn to a brief summary of each section of the book.

Prevention and Early Intervention

Overrepresentation of English language learners in special education is problematic because students without disabilities who have been referred to special education suffer negative consequences (e.g., lowered expectations for performance and reduced potential for academic, social, and economic advancement). Underrepresentation is equally troublesome because some students with disabilities are not receiving the special services that they are legally entitled to and that could help them reach their potential. In either case, federal law is violated, districts may be exposed to civil and administrative sanctions and penalties, and students may suffer irreparable harm (Rice & Ortiz, 1994).

It is the responsibility of general education programs to address the underachievement of English language learners and, at least initially, their disproportionate representation in special education programs (Artiles & Trent, 2000). In Chapter 2, "Prevention of School Failure and Early Intervention for English Language Learners," Alba Ortiz describes a 3-phase model designed to prevent school failure and provide early intervention programs for struggling learners. Phase 1 of the model prevents school failure by creating a school environment that promotes the academic success of English language learners and uses instructional strategies known to be effective for these students. Phase 2 of the model—early intervention—provides supplementary instructional services that can bring at-risk students to a level where they can benefit from instruction (Madden, Slavin, Karweit, Dolan, & Wasik, 1991). Ortiz presents three major strategies for early intervention: clinical teaching, the use of Teacher Assistance Teams (Chalfant, Pysh, & Moultrie, 1979) to help teachers design and implement programs for English language learners experiencing academic difficulties, and general education alternatives (e.g., tutoring and remedial programs) for struggling learners.

Such efforts can reduce the number of students referred to special education, the third and final phase. If this model is followed, school staff will know that a student who has been referred to special education is in all likelihood eligible for services because school efforts have exhausted the possibility that the student can remain in the general education classroom without special education support.

Assessment and Identification

While the comprehensive individual assessment provides the data upon which special education eligibility decisions are based, there is compelling evidence that traditional assessment procedures, driven by the use of norm-referenced tests, are inappropriate for English language learners. Reliance on traditional practices, even when adapted for English language learners, results in the misdiagnosis of bilingualism as a disability (Figueroa, 2000).

In Chapter 3, "Toward a New Model of Assessment," Richard Figueroa argues for shifting the paradigm from the traditional assessment model to a situated observational model. The situated model focuses on the classroom context and on identifying the conditions that result in improved teaching and learning. It builds on the pre-referral approach outlined by Ortiz in the previous chapter by linking prevention and early intervention with assessment. Figueroa contends that with enriched, effective instruction, special education services may be unnecessary. He further suggests that the role of school psychologists and educational evaluators change from that of tester to that of consultant. Under this new paradigm, assessment personnel help teachers create optimal learning environments and develop methods for collecting progress data over time to assess whether a student is profiting from instruction. Teacher documentation of students' academic difficulties, not test scores, becomes the primary criterion for determining which students receive special education services.

Until Figueroa's model is implemented, it is important to minimize biases inherent in traditionally used procedures. In Chapter 4, "Considerations in the Assessment of English Language Learners Referred to Special Education," Alba Ortiz and James Yates discuss what educators need to consider when they assess English language learners for special education services. To perform their duties effectively, assessment personnel need to understand not only standardized assessment procedures but culturally sensitive assessment procedures as well. They will need to have some understanding of first and second language acquisition theory and the impact of culture and socioeconomic status on student performance. Ortiz and Yates recommend that assessment personnel evaluate their own knowledge, skills, and beliefs to determine their qualifications to assess English language learners.

Ortiz and Yates recommend that students be assessed in their native language, as well as in English, and present strategies to assess language dominance and proficiency. This approach will help the assessment team rule out limited English proficiency as the cause of learning problems. Because of the scarcity of adequate standardized instruments for English language learners, it is important to make acceptable adaptations of existing instruments and to use multiple sources, tools, and strategies to assess the child. Assessment teams should be made up of professionals with expertise in the fields of bilingual, second language, and special education. Ideally, each member will receive training in areas outside of his or her own specialty in order to understand the perspectives and insights that other members of the team bring to the assessment process.

By assessing English language learners in their homes and communities, and involving parents as active participants in evaluations, schools can minimize misdiagnoses and inappropriate special education placements. In Chapter 5, "Parent-Professional Collaboration in Culturally Sensitive Assessment," Shernaz García first reviews the legal requirements for family participation in the assessment process. She then suggests strategies to involve families in eligibility assessments. She cautions that when the beliefs and values of parents differ from those of educators, parents may experience cultural discomfort. To help parents overcome their discomfort, professionals must first understand the cultural, linguistic, socioeconomic, and other background characteristics of the families and the students they serve. Just as important, professionals must reflect on how their own beliefs and values influence their perceptions of students and families, their interpretation of assessment data, and the instructional recommendations that they offer to support students with disabilities.

To assess students accurately and to design effective educational services for them, professionals must not only understand the family's culture but also value the "funds of knowledge" available within the family (Moll, Amanti, Neff, & González, 1992). When assessments incorporate the principle of cultural reciprocity, professionals and parents agree upon roles, share responsibilities, and enter the assessment process with a willingness to learn from each other. Cultural reciprocity is particularly important because assessment personnel too often assume the role of expert, restricting the parents' participation to that of receiver or provider of information.

Instruction

Once a student is identified as eligible for special education, the teacher then carries out the individualized education plan (IEP) by identifying what they will teach that student and how they will teach it. For English language learners, instruction needs to address both their linguistic and cultural characteristics and their disabilities.

In Chapter 6, "Culturally and Linguistically Responsive Instructional Planning," Nancy Cloud discusses the critical components of instructional planning for English language learners with disabilities. Culturally responsive teaching uses curricula and materials that take into account students' cultural backgrounds; accommodates learner differences in interpersonal interactions; selects approaches that are most compatible with learner preferences and prior experience; uses time, space, and staff in student-sensitive ways; and provides counseling and other services that are cross-culturally appropriate.

To provide effective language and literacy instruction, educators need to understand the relationship between first and second language development and the ways that disabilities affect that development. Stressing that students with disabilities benefit from dual language instruction, Cloud recommends that instruction begin by building a strong base of native language proficiency. Formal English language and literacy instruction should be introduced when it is developmentally appropriate. Through sheltered academic instruction, the language becomes understandable to the learners. Finally, Cloud stresses the importance of a family service plan that encourages the involvement of families in decision making and in the implementation of their children's instructional plans.

In Chapter 7, "Effective Pedagogy for English Language Learners in Inclusive Classrooms," Lorri Johnson Santamaría, Todd Fletcher, and

Candace Bos describe an alternative method of language arts instruction that includes *scaffolding strategies* (additional instructional support to increase student learning), effective pedagogy, and dual language instruction. Scaffolding strategies include *mediating scaffolds* that link less proficient learners with more proficient peers, *task scaffolds* that reduce the information students must generate independently, and *material scaffolds* that provide learning props that are removed over time as students become more proficient. A fourth scaffold, *comprehensible input*—language tailored to the learner's level of proficiency—is particularly important for second language learners. The authors also offer guiding principles for effective pedagogy that focus on collaborative activities, meaningful language use, and higher order thinking.

The authors then discuss two teachers who incorporated scaffolding strategies and the principles of instruction in their third-grade bilingual education classes. The teachers' uses of scaffolds enabled students to learn content in their primary language before attempting similar tasks in English. The instructional strategies of these teachers corroborate the authors' guiding principles for instruction. These strategies and principles hold tremendous promise for promoting effective pedagogy for English language learners in both general and special education.

In Chapter 8, "Walking the Talk: The Joys and Challenges of Critical Pedagogy," Barbara Goldstein presents a thoughtful discussion of Freire's pedagogy of the oppressed in relation to English language learners with disabilities. Goldstein profiles two bilingual educators and their attempts to practice critical pedagogy with English language learners, both with and without special needs, in their elementary classes.

According to Goldstein, teachers who use critical pedagogy empower students by making the relationships of power and privilege explicit and understandable to students and their families and by providing meaningful contexts for language, literacy, and content area instruction. She describes key features of critical pedagogy in elementary settings. This discussion, which mirrors the recommendations provided by Cloud and by Santamaría, Fletcher, and Bos, centers on five themes:

interactive student-centered instructional practices, multiple opportunities for students to develop language and academic skills, emergent curriculum that connects personal experience to community concerns and global issues, collaboration with parents and community, and the personal and professional challenges that critical educators face as they struggle to survive with hope and integrity.

Goldstein stresses that it is important for educators to do what is in the best interests of students by supporting programs and services that are often unpopular (e.g., bilingual education and bilingual special education). She states, "Teaching is challenging work, and when one is working within a system that is diametrically opposed to one's beliefs, ideas, and vision of possibilities, the challenge can become oppressive" (pp. 178–179). She ends her chapter with suggestions for ways that teachers can reduce stress and build support systems that relieve the sense of isolation that critical educators often experience.

Trends and Future Directions

In the concluding chapter, "Educating English Language Learners With Special Needs: Trends and Future Directions," Leonard Baca, one of the founders of the bilingual special education field, reflects on major issues and charts future directions for the field. According to Baca, the two central issues facing the field are assessment (are we identifying the right students?) and instruction (are we providing appropriate instruction?). Baca argues that the population served by bilingual special education is forcing the field to transcend its traditional exclusive focus on children's deficits. He concludes by arguing that we need to redefine the basic tenets and assumptions that inform research and practice in the field of special education for English language learners.

Given the growing numbers of English language learners in our schools and the inclusive education movement, this book will be of interest to a wide range of K–12 educators. It will help educators better understand the issues that they face in their efforts to educate a population of

English language learners whose unique needs have been largely c
looked. The ultimate goal of this book, however, is practical: to provide
professionals who work with these students useful and effective strategies to address their complex cultural, linguistic, and learning needs.

Author's Note:
Alfredo J. Artiles acknowledges the support of the COMRISE Project at
the University of Virginia under grant #H029J60006 awarded by the
U.S. Department of Education, Office of Special Education Programs.

Prevention and Early Intervention

Prevention of School Failure and Early Intervention for English Language Learners

Alba A. Ortiz, *University of Texas at Austin*

While students fail in school for a variety of reasons (Adelman, 1970; García & Ortiz, 1988; Ortiz, 1997; Ortiz & Wilkinson, 1991), it is possible to distinguish among three broad categories of students who experience serious academic difficulty. Type I students fail because of deficiencies in the teaching-learning environment. For example, students learning English are likely to fail when they do not have access to effective bilingual education or English as a second language (ESL) programs, and those from lower socioeconomic environments may fail if instruction assumes middle-class experiences and regards departure from such norms as deviance.

Type II students experience academic difficulties that cannot be attributed to a learning disability. For example, students who are reading below grade level because of excessive absences will not become effective readers unless instruction is individualized or they have access to remedial reading programs. Students who are promoted from one grade without having mastered the curriculum will have difficulty in the next grade because they lack knowledge or skills essential for that grade. Unless their learning problems are addressed, these students will continue to struggle, and the gap between their achievement and that of their peers will widen over time. Referring Type II students to special education is inappropriate because their continued difficulty can be explained by the school system's failure to intervene in a timely and effective manner.

Type III students are those who have been evaluated and found to have disabilities such as mental retardation, speech or language disorders, emotional disturbances, or learning disabilities. These students require special education and related services designed to meet their unique needs (Individuals With Disabilities Act Amendments, 1997). The over-representation of English language learners in special education (Robertson, Kushner, Starks, & Drescher, 1994; Yates & Ortiz, 1998b) suggests that educators have difficulty distinguishing Type III students—those who truly have disabilities—from Type I and Type II students, who are failing for other reasons (Ortiz et al., 1985; Ortiz, García, Wheeler, & Maldonado-Colón, 1986).

The root of academic problems experienced by Type I and Type II students is presumed to be in the environments and conditions surrounding the teaching-learning process, not in the child (García & Ortiz, 1988; Ortiz & Wilkinson, 1991). Hodgkinson (1993) wonders why, if we know which students are at the highest risk of school failure, we do not focus attention and target resources on improving the education system to better serve these learners.

> If we were told that an unfriendly foreign power had disabled one-third of our youth, rendering them incapable of reasonable performance in school, we would view it as an act of war. We don't need to imagine a foreign enemy; by systematically neglecting the needs and potential of disadvantaged children, we have done the damage to ourselves. (p. 623)

This chapter discusses the overrepresentation of English language learners in special education and the responsibility of the general education system to address this problem. Preventing academic failure requires school improvement efforts and early intervention programs for struggling learners. When the general education system responds effectively to the unique learning needs of English language learners, fewer will have to be referred to special education. In all likelihood, those who are referred will be eligible for services because prevention and early intervention efforts will have exhausted the possibility that the students can be maintained in general education classes without special education support.

Phase I: Prevention of School Failure Among English Language Learners

Prevention of failure among English language learners involves two critical elements (see Figure 1): the creation of educational environments conducive to academic success (Madden, Slavin, Karweit, Dolan, & Wasik, 1991) and the use of instructional strategies known to be effective with these students (Ortiz, 1997; Ortiz & Wilkinson, 1991).

Positive School Climates

Preventing school failure begins with creating school climates that foster academic success (Cummins, 1989; Stedman, 1987). Such environments reflect a philosophy that all students can learn and, perhaps more importantly, that educators are responsible for seeing to it that they do. Positive school climates are characterized by strong leadership by principals; high expectations for student achievement; a challenging curriculum; a safe and orderly environment; ongoing, systematic evaluation of student progress; and the involvement of administrators, teachers, community members, and parents in school governance and decision making (Anderson & Pellicer, 1998; Walberg, Bakalis, Bast, & Baer, 1989).

FIGURE **1** ▪

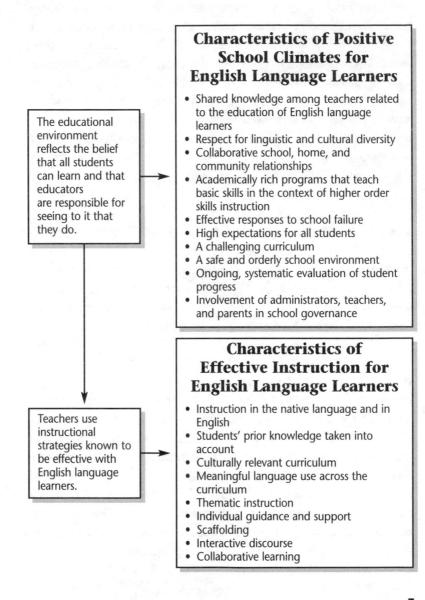

The educational environment reflects the belief that all students can learn and that educators are responsible for seeing to it that they do.

Characteristics of Positive School Climates for English Language Learners

- Shared knowledge among teachers related to the education of English language learners
- Respect for linguistic and cultural diversity
- Collaborative school, home, and community relationships
- Academically rich programs that teach basic skills in the context of higher order skills instruction
- Effective responses to school failure
- High expectations for all students
- A challenging curriculum
- A safe and orderly school environment
- Ongoing, systematic evaluation of student progress
- Involvement of administrators, teachers, and parents in school governance

Teachers use instructional strategies known to be effective with English language learners.

Characteristics of Effective Instruction for English Language Learners

- Instruction in the native language and in English
- Students' prior knowledge taken into account
- Culturally relevant curriculum
- Meaningful language use across the curriculum
- Thematic instruction
- Individual guidance and support
- Scaffolding
- Interactive discourse
- Collaborative learning

Phase I: Prevention of School Failure

These factors affect the academic success of all students; several other factors specifically affect the success of English language learners. These include (a) a shared knowledge base among educators who serve English language learners, (b) an acceptance and understanding of linguistic and cultural diversity, (c) collaborative school and community relationships, (d) academically rich programs that teach basic skills in the context of higher order skills in both the native language and in English, and (e) the elimination of ineffective responses to failure (Cummins, 1989; Ortiz, 1997; Ortiz & Wilkinson, 1991; Stedman, 1987).

A Shared Knowledge Base

Most general and special education teachers do not have extensive coursework or training related to the education of learners from culturally and linguistically diverse backgrounds (García, 1992; Kushner & Ortiz, 2000); fewer still have been trained to understand the specific needs of English language learners. This lack of knowledge on the part of teachers helps to explain the poor academic performance of these students. Therefore, professional development activities must ensure that teachers share a common philosophy and knowledge base concerning the education of learners from culturally and linguistically diverse backgrounds (García, Wilkinson, & Ortiz, 1995; Wang, Reynolds, & Walberg, 1995). Given the growing diversity of our student population, *all* teachers, regardless of teaching assignment, should have training in second language acquisition and the relationship of the native language to the development of English proficiency, first and second language teaching methodology, sociocultural influences on learning, assessment of proficiency in the first language and in English, informal assessment strategies to monitor progress, and strategies for working with culturally and linguistically diverse families and communities.

Acceptance of Linguistic and Cultural Diversity

In schools with positive educational climates, special language programs enjoy the support of principals, teachers, parents, and community members. Arguments about bilingual education have been laid to rest because school staff share a common understanding about the education of English language learners. It is understood that native language instruction provides the foundation for achieving high levels of English proficiency (Cummins, 1984; Krashen, 1982a, 1991; Thomas & Collier, 1997). Thus, using the native language is a key instructional strategy in these schools (Snow, Burns, & Griffin, 1998). It is also clearly understood that general education teachers are critical to the success of English language learners and that language development is a shared responsibility and not the sole purview of bilingual and ESL teachers.

The majority of English language learners are served in ESL programs, not in bilingual education, and thus do not receive native language instruction (August & Hakuta, 1997). Students typically receive ESL support on a pull-out basis, usually for an hour a day, spending the rest of their time in general education classes (Cummins, 1994b). Even those who benefit from bilingual education often exit these programs before they have developed the English skills needed to compete successfully with native-English-speaking peers (Cummins, 1981). It can be argued, then, that general education teachers have as much responsibility for helping the English language learners in their classes acquire English as a second language as do ESL teachers. In practice, though, the reverse is true: ESL teachers are often given the unrealistic, if not impossible, task of teaching English as a second language, literacy, and the content areas—in 1 to 2 hours a day.

In effective schools, all teachers use ESL strategies, a byproduct of the professional development provided to create a shared knowledge base among teachers. For example, as a way of making instruction comprehensible to learners (Krashen, 1982a, 1991), they scaffold learning by using advance organizers and concrete referents or visuals, by teaching key vocabulary and main ideas, and by providing periodic reviews of important concepts. Teachers integrate language and academic content instruction, thus providing opportunities for students to develop academic language proficiency (Cummins, 1984; Ortiz & García, 1990; Willig, Swedo, & Ortiz, 1987). General education teachers, working in collaboration with ESL colleagues, help students achieve native-like levels of English proficiency.

In schools with positive climates, teachers are also aware that their own culture influences their views of the teaching-learning process and shapes the classroom culture (García & Dominguez, 1997; Ortiz, 1997). They make sure that students see themselves—their life experiences, language, culture, norms, values, and physical attributes—in the curriculum (Taylor, 2000). They do so by using instructional materials that are free of stereotypes; by presenting both minority and majority perspectives; and by acknowledging the contemporary social, political, and economic experiences of their students (García & Dominguez, 1997; García & Malkin, 1993; Santos, Fowler, Corso, & Bruns, 2000). At the same time, students learn to interact successfully with members of cultures different from their own and to negotiate the classroom and school cultures successfully.

Collaborative School-Community Relationships

Some educators believe that parents of children at risk of failing in school cannot or will not provide their children what they need and that professionals must "correct" child-rearing practices and provide young children with "appropriate" experiences (Lubeck, 1994). In contrast, in schools with positive climates, parents from culturally and linguistically diverse backgrounds are seen as effective advocates for their children and as valuable resources in school improvement efforts (Cummins, 1989, 1994b; García, this volume; García & Malkin, 1993; Santos, Fowler, Corso, & Bruns, 2000). By being involved with the families and communities of English language learners, educators come to understand the social, linguistic, and cultural contexts in which their students are raised (Anderson & Pellicer, 1998; García, this volume; García & Dominguez, 1997; Ortiz, 1997). Thus, educators learn to respect cultural differences in child-rearing practices and in how parents choose to be involved in their children's education (García, this volume; García & Dominguez, 1997). They relinquish control over decision making and join parents and other community members in promoting academic progress at both school and at home (Cummins, 1989; García, this volume; García, Wilkinson, & Ortiz, 1995). According to Cummins (1989), "When educators involve minority parents as partners in their children's education, parents appear to develop a sense of advocacy that communicates itself to children—with positive academic consequences" (p. 114).

Academically Rich Programs

Another possible explanation for the bleak outcomes of schooling for students from culturally and linguistically diverse backgrounds is the focus in school on lower level basic skills. While current education reforms emphasize higher order skills and a challenging curriculum, curriculum and instruction for struggling learners continue to emphasize lower level basic skills (Cummins, 1984; Elmore & Fuhrman, 1994; Knapp, Shields, & Turnbull, 1995; Oakes, 1986; Ortiz, 1997; Ortiz & Wilkinson, 1991). Yet research indicates that an emphasis on basic skills is misguided:

> These approaches emphasize curricula that proceed in a linear fashion from the "basics" to "advanced" skills (though seldom reaching the latter), instruction that is tightly controlled by the teacher and ability grouping that often hardens into permanent tracks at an early age. . . . Although these approaches may improve children's grasp of basic skills (and there is evidence that they do), they risk shortchanging the learning of more advanced skills in comprehension, reasoning, and composition. (Knapp, Shields, & Turnbull, 1995, p. 771)

Struggling learners are better served by curricula and instruction that nest basic skill instruction in the context of higher order thinking and problem solving (Cummins, 1984; Ortiz & Wilkinson, 1991; Willig, Swedo, & Ortiz, 1987). For example, reading instruction can emphasize comprehension but also include lessons on phonics and word recognition. Teachers can use writing approaches that emphasize communication of ideas in a well-organized, coherent fashion but also teach mechanics such as spelling, grammar, and punctuation (Ortiz & Wilkinson, 1991).

Elimination of Ineffective Responses to School Failure

Retention in grade, low-ability grouping, and special education placement are common responses to the academic problems of Type I and Type II students (Garcia & Ortiz, 1988; Knapp, Shields, & Turnbull, 1995; Ortiz & Wilkinson, 1991). These low-performing students often spend most of their school day together, which results in de facto tracking or segregation (Knapp, Shields, & Turnbull, 1995). Over time, they come to believe that they cannot master challenging academic content. This belief in turn lowers their self-esteem, diminishes their interest in school and their motivation to do well, and contributes to high dropout rates (Ortiz & Kushner, 1997).

The scarcity of appropriate assessment instruments and of personnel trained to conduct culturally and linguistically relevant assessments puts English language learners at a disadvantage (Valdés & Figueroa, 1994). Students who qualify for special education are further disadvantaged by the shortage of special educators trained to address their limited English proficiency and disability-related needs simultaneously (Ortiz, 1997; Ortiz & Wilkinson, 1991; Yates & Ortiz, 1991). Some educators argue that if general education teachers have given up on failing students, special education support is better than no help at all. Too often, however, the hope that special education will close achievement gaps is not realized. For example, reevaluations of Hispanic students who had been in special education for 3 years showed that their IQ scores were lower than at initial placement and that their achievement scores were essentially the same as at entry (Wilkinson & Ortiz, 1986). This is disturbing given the likelihood that some of these youngsters were actually Type I or Type II students; neither general education nor special education met their needs. High expectations and academically rich programs can improve the academic achievement of English language learners, but only if students receive high-quality instruction designed to meet those expectations (O'Day & Smith, cited in Smith, Furhman, & O'Day, 1994).

Effective Instruction

In classes where English language learners are successful, teachers use instructional strategies known to be effective for learners from culturally and linguistically diverse backgrounds (Ortiz & Wilkinson, 1991; Willig, Swedo, & Ortiz, 1987). They draw heavily upon students' prior knowledge, linking what students already know to what they need to learn (Brophy, 1992; Leinhardt, 1992). They provide multiple opportunities for students to review previously learned concepts, and they teach students to apply those concepts to the tasks at hand (Burke, Hagan, & Grossen, 1998). They organize the content into themes that connect the curriculum across subject areas.

Because struggling learners often lack the skills to complete tasks successfully, teachers provide individual guidance, assistance, and support to fill in gaps in background knowledge (Brophy, 1992; Burke, Hagan, & Grossen, 1998). This type of scaffolding helps students make the transition from teacher-directed to self-directed learning (Burke, Hagan, & Grossen, 1998; see Santamaría, Fletcher, & Bos, this volume, for a discussion of the use of scaffolding strategies with English language learners). As their skills improve, students begin regulating their own learning and assume greater levels of responsibility and independence (Leinhardt, 1992). The teacher becomes a guide or facilitator (Cummins, 1984).

Ideal instructional activities for English language learners allow genuine dialogue between teachers and students and among students as they work on assignments that encourage them to question and discuss (Cummins, 1984; Fillmore & Valadez, 1986; Leinhardt, 1992; Willig, Swedo, & Ortiz, 1987). Collaborative learning activities facilitate task engagement and provide opportunities to to use language for both conversational and academic purposes and to practice language skills (McGroarty, 1989; Willig, Swedo, & Ortiz, 1987).

In summary, establishing a positive school climate and ensuring that students receive effective instruction are the most cost-effective means of improving academic achievement and preventing at-risk students from falling further behind (Fashola & Slavin, 1998; Ortiz, 1997; Ortiz & Wilkinson, 1991). In the absence of such a climate, educators will find themselves in a never-ending cycle of remediation because the educational system itself continues to engender student failure.

Phase II: Early Intervention for Struggling Learners

Although most learning problems can be prevented in schools and classes that accommodate individual differences, even in the most positive environments some students still experience serious difficulty (Fashola & Slavin, 1998; Ortiz, 1997; Ortiz & Kushner, 1997). For these students, early intervention strategies must be implemented *as soon as learning problems are noted* (see Figure 2). Early intervention means that "supplementary instructional services are provided early in students' schooling and that they are intense enough to bring at-risk students quickly to a level at which they can profit from high-quality classroom instruction" (Madden, Slavin, Karweit, Dolan, & Wasik, 1991, p. 594).

In discussing Phase II, the term *early intervention* is used instead of *pre-referral intervention.* Historically, the purpose of pre-referral intervention has been to prevent unnecessary special education referrals and placements (Fuchs, Fuchs, Bahr, Fernstrom, & Stecker, 1990; García & Ortiz, 1988). All too often, though, pre-referral activities occur too late to be effective in distinguishing Type I and Type II from Type III students. By the time teachers request pre-referral assistance, their interest in problem solving may be half-hearted and with good reason. Research shows that if students are more than a year below grade level for their age, even the best remedial or special education programs are unlikely to succeed (Slavin & Madden, 1989). Teachers have come to view pre-referral intervention as a hurdle they have to jump before their students are tested for special education. However, the failure of educators in the general education program to intervene in a timely

FIGURE **2** ■

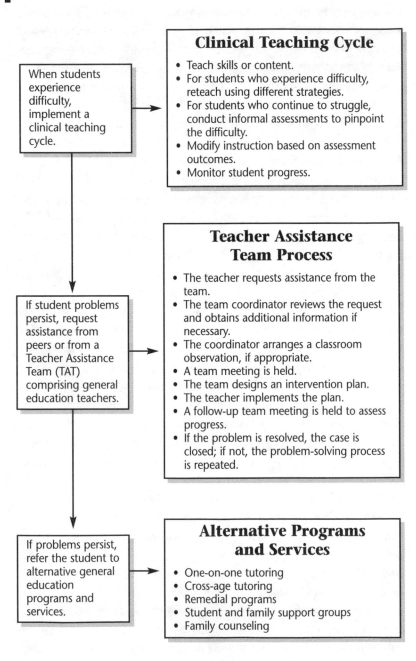

Phase II: Early Intervention for Struggling Learners

fashion, not the presence of a disability, may be the real source of the students' difficulties. Thus, the intent of Phase II is to create timely and effective general education support that improves the academic performance of struggling learners and, as a result, reduces inappropriate special education referrals.

Examples of early intervention include clinical teaching; general education peer and teacher support; and alternative general education services, such as tutorial or remedial instruction (Ortiz, 1997; Ortiz & Wilkinson, 1991). Each of these is described below. These interventions should be initiated as soon as a teacher notices that a student is experiencing academic difficulties, not when learning problems have become so serious that the teacher has decided that the student should be referred to special education.

Clinical Teaching

Clinical teaching is instruction that is carefully sequenced. Teachers teach skills, subjects, or concepts; reteach the material using different strategies or approaches for the benefit of students who fail to meet expected performance levels after initial instruction; and use informal assessment strategies to identify students' strengths and weaknesses and the possible causes of academic difficulties (Adelman, 1970; García & Ortiz, 1988; Ortiz, 1997; Ortiz & Wilkinson, 1991). Teachers conduct curriculum-based assessments (e.g., by using observations, inventories, and analyses of student work) to monitor student progress and use data from these assessments to plan and modify instruction (King-Sears, Burgess, & Lawson, 1999; Tucker, 1985).

In the case of English language learners, assessing conversational and academic language proficiency is critical to deciding the language(s) of instruction and determining the learning goals and objectives for language instruction (Cummins, 1984; Ortiz & García, 1990). Assessment data, along with documentation of efforts to improve student performance, are invaluable when students are referred to remedial or special education programs (García & Ortiz, 1988; Ortiz, 1997; Ortiz & Kushner, 1997).

Peer Support and Teacher Assistance Teams

When clinical teaching is unsuccessful, teachers should have immediate access to general education support systems for further problem solving (Chalfant & Pysh, 1989; Chalfant, Pysh, & Moultrie, 1979). Two examples of such supports are peer or expert consultation (Fashola & Slavin, 1998; Fuchs et al., 1990) and Teacher Assistance Teams (Chalfant, Pysh, & Moultrie, 1979).

Peer or Expert Consultation

Peers or experts can work collaboratively with general education teachers to develop strategies to address students' learning problems and to guide the teachers as they implement recommendations (Fuchs at al., 1990). For example, teachers can share instructional resources and can observe each other's classrooms and offer suggestions for improving instruction or managing behavior. ESL teachers can help their general education peers by demonstrating strategies for successfully integrating English language learners into their classes; general education and ESL teachers can meet to coordinate ESL and content instruction. In schools with positive climates, faculty function as a community and share the goal of helping students and each other, regardless of the labels students have been given or the program or classes to which teachers or students are assigned.

The Teacher Assistance Team (TAT)

The Teacher Assistance Team (TAT) (Chalfant, Pysh, & Moultrie, 1979) can help teachers resolve problems that they routinely encounter in their classes. The TAT, made up of four to six general education teachers and the teacher who requests assistance, designs intervention strategies to help struggling learners. Other individuals (e.g., administrators, special educators, assessment personnel, and parents) may be invited to meet with the team as needed. For example, it would be appropriate to invite the school nurse to join the team if members suspect that health issues are affecting student learning. If a divorce is causing the child stress, then the presence of the parents or a school counselor would be helpful.

At the TAT meeting, team members reach consensus on the nature of the problem; determine priorities for intervention; help the teacher select the methods, strategies, or approaches to be used in solving the problem; assign responsibility for carrying out the recommendations; and establish a follow-up plan to monitor progress (Chalfant, Pysh, & Moultrie, 1979). The teacher then implements the plan, with the assistance of team members or other colleagues, if needed. Follow-up meetings are held to review progress toward problem resolution. If the problem is resolved, the case is closed; if not, the team repeats the problem-solving process.

It is important to understand that when teachers contact the team, they are requesting assistance from the TAT for themselves; they are not referring students to the team. In other words, they do not wish to transfer responsibility for student learning to someone else. They continue to "own the problem" and seek to resolve it with the assistance of peers. This distinguishes the TAT process from the typical pre-referral intervention, which is too often initiated because the teacher wants the child removed from general education classes and placed in special education for at least part of the day.

Serving on the TAT is an excellent professional development activity for team members and especially for teachers who request assistance from the team. The next time they encounter a student with a problem similar to one that the team helped to resolve, they know what to do. An additional benefit is that the TAT coordinator can analyze the types of problems for which teachers requested assistance and share this information with the principal (without identifying the teachers who requested assistance). This allows the principal to identify issues that need to be addressed on a broader scale (e.g., the need to revise the school's discipline plan or to implement a tutoring program) or professional development topics that could benefit the entire faculty (e.g., how to determine when students are truly English proficient or when to move students from reading in the native language to reading in English).

Research on TATs has shown that general education teachers on these teams have the skills and competencies to work with students with serious learning needs and that the majority of cases considered by teams are resolved without referral to special education (Chalfant & Pysh, 1989; Ortiz, 1990). Given this, limiting membership in TATs to general educators gives specialists more time to spend on tasks for which they are uniquely prepared—for example, conducting assessments or consulting with general education teachers to implement inclusive education programs.

Alternative Services

General education, not special education, should be primarily responsible for the education of students with special learning needs that cannot be attributed to disabilities. These would include migrant students who miss critical instruction over the course of the school year or immigrant children who arrive in U.S. schools without prior education. If the general education system does not have alternatives for students such as these, teachers and principals tend to conclude that it is in the students' best interest to refer them to special education (Frymier & Gansnedner, 1989).

A variety of general education alternatives exists for students with special needs. These include one-on-one and cross-age tutoring, family and student support groups, family counseling, and the range of services supported by Title I funds. Support provided to students through these programs supplements, rather than replaces, general education instruction (Slavin & Madden, 1989). Moreover, services should be intensive and temporary, and students who are removed from their regular classes for supplemental instruction should be returned to those classes as quickly as possible (Anderson & Pellicer, 1998; Slavin & Madden, 1989).

Phase III: Referral to Special Education

Prevention and early intervention are not intended to discourage special education referrals. Rather, they are meant to prevent the referral of students whose problems result from factors other than the presence of a disability. When Phase I and II activities fail to resolve learning difficulties, then referral to special education is warranted (see Figure 3).

The responsibilities of special education referral committees are similar to those of Teacher Assistance Teams. The primary difference is that, in addition to general education teachers, referral committees include a variety of specialists, including principals, special education teachers, and assessment personnel. These specialists bring their expertise to bear on the problem, especially in areas related to assessment, diagnosis, and specialized instruction.

FIGURE **3** ■

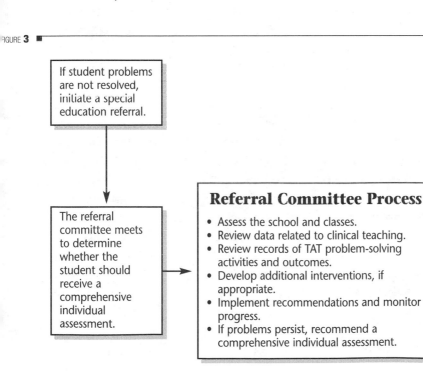

Referral Committee Process

- Assess the school and classes.
- Review data related to clinical teaching.
- Review records of TAT problem-solving activities and outcomes.
- Develop additional interventions, if appropriate.
- Implement recommendations and monitor progress.
- If problems persist, recommend a comprehensive individual assessment.

Phase III: Referral to Special Education

Decisions of the referral committee are informed by data gathered through the prevention, early intervention, and referral processes (Ortiz, 1997). The recommendation that a student receive a comprehensive individual assessment indicates that the child is in a positive school climate, that the teacher used instructional strategies known to be effective for English language learners, that neither clinical teaching nor intervention strategies recommended by the Teacher Assistance Team resolved the problem, and that other general education alternatives also proved unsuccessful. It is likely that students who continue to struggle, in spite of such extensive efforts to individualize instruction and to accommodate learning characteristics, have disabilities (García & Ortiz, 1988; Ortiz, 1997; Ortiz & Wilkinson, 1991).

Conclusion

Prevention of school failure and early intervention to correct students' academic difficulties are, first and foremost, the responsibility of general education professionals. If school climates are not supportive, and if instruction in general education is not tailored to meet the needs of students from culturally and linguistically diverse backgrounds, English language learners have little chance of succeeding. Intervention strategies that focus solely on remediating students' learning and behavior problems will yield limited results because the school and classroom contexts necessary to maintain high academic achievement are absent.

Prevention and early intervention efforts can significantly improve the academic achievement of English language learners. These efforts will reduce the number of students at risk of failing, of being inaccurately identified as having a disability, and of being inappropriately referred to remedial or special education programs. These outcomes are critical given the concern that as our schools become more diverse, the special education system may become overwhelmed by students whose needs have not been met by the general education system.

Assessment and Identification

Toward a New Model of Assessment

Richard A. Figueroa, *University of California, Davis*

Twelve years ago, Figueroa (1990) recommended a series of steps for school psychologists to consider in assessing an English language learner for special education services. These steps included assessing the effectiveness of the instructional program, the family's cultural background, the learner's proficiencies in the first and second languages, and the learner's intelligence. Framed against the historical, empirical literature in the United States on the schooling and testing of English language learners, the recommendations considered court decisions on minority overrepresentation in special education and professional standards on testing English language learners (American Educational Research Association, 1985).

The fundamental message to diagnosticians who assess English language learners for special education services was that their practices were flawed and not supported by empirical evidence. Breaking ranks with the traditional, test-driven paradigm that undergirds professional assessment practices in special education, Figueroa (1990) recommended that assessment personnel rely more on classroom observations than on tests or test-like procedures. To this end, he proposed three key principles: Observe the English language learner's behavior and functioning in multiple contexts, observe longitudinally, and rely principally on informed professional judgment in reaching diagnostic conclusions.

In "Best Practices in Working With Bilingual Children," López (1995) suggested that assessment professionals consider 14 areas for diagnostic work and treatment. López made 86 recommendations for collecting information in order to validly assess and teach English language learners who had been referred for special education placement. This massive amount of data collection suggests three things: The English language learner is an extremely complex entity, the current technology and professional practices for carrying out diagnostic work in special education may not be adequate for English language learners (hence the need for 86 recommendations), and the testing paradigm for students who are referred for special education placement may not work with English language learners.

It is not possible in this chapter to review the literature on the diagnostic assessment of English language learners (Abedi, 1999a, 1999b, 1999c, 2000; Abedi, Hoffstetter, Baker, & Lord, 1998; Abedi, Lord, & Hoffstetter, 1998; Abedi, Lord, & Plummer, 1995; August & Hakuta, 1997; Figueroa, 2000; Figueroa & Hernandez, 2000; Heubert & Hauser, 1999; Pellegrino, Jones, & Mitchell, 1999; Shakrani, 1999; Valdés & Figueroa, 1994). This literature suggests that the practice of traditional norm-referenced testing with this population may no longer be tenable. Accordingly, this chapter makes the following new recommendations: Change the paradigm for assessing English language learners, observe underachieving learners in enriched instructional contexts, and improve the referral and placement process.

Changing the Paradigm
The Old Paradigm

Kuhn's (1970) analysis of scientific revolutions showed how scientific reality—how scientists thought about what they thought about (Poplin, 1988)—changed when inconsistent results and outcomes could no longer be explained by an existing approach to knowledge. A viable argument can be made that this is exactly where diagnosis in special education currently finds itself when it concerns English language learners.

The overrepresentation of English language learners in special education programs is well documented (see discussion in Artiles & Ortiz, this volume). It is unclear, however, whether this overrepresentation is the result of actual learner disabilities or whether it is the result of testing procedures that cannot distinguish between disability and bilingualism as causes of learning difficulties (Figueroa, 2000; Figueroa & Hernandez, 2000; Valdés & Figueroa, 1994).

Research has documented the disruptive impact of bilingualism on psychometric test properties. Predictive validity (how well a test predicts future performance) may be compromised by home language backgrounds other than English (Figueroa & García, 1994; Jensen, 1980). In addition, construct validity (how well a test measures what it is supposed to measure) is disrupted (Jensen, 1976), and reliability (how consistently a test measures the same thing) is diminished (Abedi, 2000).

Even with assessments that measure discrete skills, such as how well children can repeat numbers forward and backwards, factors associated with bilingualism alter what is normally observed in monolingual speakers. Since the early part of the 20th century, researchers have noticed that English language learners (who are to some degree bilingual) find it easier than monolingual English speakers to recall numbers in reverse order than to remember them in the exact order presented (Darsie, 1926; Hung-Hsia, 1929; Jensen & Inouye, 1980; Luh & Wy, 1931; Manuel, 1935). This small fact alone can have a considerable effect on how learning disabilities are diagnosed with English language learners. Typically, digit span scores (recalling numbers) serve to document the presence of a processing disorder in children with symptoms of a learning disability. These scores also serve to document memory or attention deficits in monolingual students. But they fail to do so for English language learners, for whom low test scores can be ascribed to the well-established finding that processing information in the second language is a slower, more fragile process (American Educational Research Association, 1985, 1999; Dornic, 1977, 1978, 1979). Further, while this slower processing of information may hinder the ability of bilingual children to recall numbers in order, it may actually help their ability to recall numbers in the reverse order (Valdés & Figueroa, 1994).

Even the accommodations used historically in assessing bilingual students have been discredited. For example, the use of interpreters, which remains popular to the present, may be invalid. In what may be the most well-controlled study on the use of interpreters during diagnostic testing, Sanchez-Boyce (2000) found that this practice adversely affects validity and reliability in the assessment of bilingual children. She analyzed 10 diagnostic testing sessions that were conducted by either a school psychologist or a speech and language clinician using an interpreter. Among many other findings, Sanchez-Boyce found that the directions related to test set up and administration were often not followed when an interpreter was used. The complexities of the communication patterns as two adults shifted from one language to the other when testing a child overwhelmed standardized procedures. This basically means that the test scores and the subsequent diagnoses based on them were not valid. The decisions reached in this process were social constructions, not diagnostic findings of a learning disability, mental retardation, or speech and language impairments. They were more like guesses.

Sanchez-Boyce's (2000) findings suggest that monolingual English-speaking school psychologists, speech and language therapists, and other special education diagnosticians have only two choices for working with English language learners: Become highly proficient bilinguals or look for another way to determine why some English language learners do not make satisfactory academic progress.

In a similar vein, it can be empirically demonstrated that the use of translated tests, no matter how well done (for example, with back translations going from English to a Spanish translation and then translated back into English), should be disallowed (Figueroa & Hernandez,

2000; Valdés & Figueroa, 1994). Rigorous attempts to produce psychometrically valid and comparable dual-language versions of tests have concluded that the effort may well be impossible (Anderson, & Olson, 1996; Olson & Goldstein, 1997).

Consider one of the tests most widely used with bilingual students, the Woodcock-Johnson Pyschoeducational Battery-Revised (Woodcock & Johnson, 1989) and the Batería Woodcock-Muñoz-Revisada (Woodcock & Muñoz-Sandoval, 1996). As described in the technical manual of the Batería (Chacon, 1999; Figueroa, 2000; Valdés & Figueroa, 1994), the sampling norms are a composite of Spanish speakers from seven countries (including speakers from five states in the United States). Apart from providing insufficient demographic and socioeconomic data about the sampling norms, this "bilingual" test assumes that the school experiences of all of the subjects are comparable. It also assumes that lexical and semantic variations across these countries are insignificant in a testing situation in which contextual clues are deliberately diminished, if not excluded.

A critical assumption of many test makers and users is that it is possible to test an English language learner as long as the same test is available in the learner's first and second language. Typically, such tests have norms for each language. Monolingual norms may not be appropriate for a child in the process of becoming bilingual, however (Grosjean, 1989). In fact, data suggest that testing English language learners in the native language produces unexplained outcomes. In an important study that used psychometric tests developed for Spanish speakers, Rueda and his colleagues (Rueda, Figueroa, Mercado, & Cardoza, 1984) found that of English language learners who had not been referred for special education, the tests misdiagnosed 47% with learning disabilities and 7% with mental retardation. Among those students diagnosed by the school system as learning disabled, the study found that only 38% were actually learning disabled, and a diagnosis of mental retardation was confirmed for only 58% of the English language learners placed in programs for students with mental retardation. In effect, using assessments normed in either the native language or in English with English language learners may produce diagnoses that cannot be defended.

The empirical evidence strongly suggests, therefore, that testing and assessment practices now in use in special education do not benefit English language learners. Given the current research on the bias of tests with English language learners (Abedi, 1999a, 1999b, 1999c, 2000; Abedi, Hoffstetter, Baker, & Lord, 1998; Abedi, Lord, & Hoffstetter, 1998; Abedi, Lord, & Plummer, 1995; Figueroa & García, 1994; Figueroa & Hernandez, 2000; Shakrani, 1999), the continued use of these tests by school systems may lead to new forms of judicial complaints.

Toward a New Paradigm

What would a revolutionary change mean for a special education diagnostician? Currently, special education assessments assume that it is possible to diagnose a learning disability much like a doctor diagnoses a medical condition. Based on a set of tests and procedures, a determination is made about the existence of a disability and about the inner mental processing capabilities of a given student. Once a disability is diagnosed, a treatment plan is prescribed.

A paradigm shift, or a fundamental change, would be somewhat heretical given historical testing practices. Suppose that it is not important to know whether there is a disability in order to help an English language learner learn. Suppose that it is not necessary to have an assessment before there can be effective instruction. Suppose that children with disabilities and without disabilities learn in fundamentally the same manner, and that the only difference is that those with disabilities may require more support in the classroom. Instruction for English language learners who are struggling in school could be offered simply on the basis of how they do in class rather than on how they perform on tests that may not even be able to assess their capabilities.

A new paradigm would require that testers rely more on observing English language learners than on testing them. The question is where they should be observed. While the literature (Figueroa, 1990; López, 1995) recommends that students be observed in multiple contexts (e.g., family and community contexts), little guidance is given as to how these observations will inform the fundamental question: Why are they not learning? Further, the time involved in conducting the recommended observations would preclude assessing more than a few learners per year.

The National Academy of Sciences, in its report on racial and ethnic overrepresentation in special education (Heller, Holtzman, & Messick, 1982), made an important recommendation that points to a solution: Before assessing a child for special education, first assess the instructional program. From new research on effective instructional practices (Tharp, 1997) and on the relationship between second language acquisition and academic achievement (Gándara, 1999), it is now possible to make a recommendation: Determining why an English language learner is not progressing can best be done by observing the child in an enriched, effective classroom. There, it is possible to distinguish learning problems that can be attributed to a deficiency in the teaching and learning environment from problems that can be attributed to disabilities (García & Ortiz, 1988). The classroom is the best place to determine what works, what does not work, and what is needed in order to "cure" learning problems. The research on this is nascent and quite promising (Enguidanos & Ruiz, 1997; Graves, Valles, & Rueda, 2000; Ruiz & Enguidanos, 1997; Ruiz & Figueroa, 1995).

Creating Enriched Instructional Environments

The current national emphasis on raising standards for all students and on accountability may provide clear documentation that special education is often ineffective, even though for years we have had ample evidence of high school noncompletion, underemployment, poverty, and marginalization among special education students after they leave high school (Guy, Hasazi, & Johnson, 1999). Similarly, a robust and compelling literature has documented over and over again the flaws of the special education system (Mehan, Hartweck, & Meihls, 1986; Mercer, 1973; Poplin, 1988; Skrtic, 1991, 1995).

Ironically, another body of work documents the efficacy of special education, provided it remains faithful to the tenets of behaviorism, skill development, and strict pedagogical regimentation (e.g., Swanson, 1999, 2000). This empirical literature, however, has little relevance for English language learners, who were not included in the published studies on the effectiveness of special education interventions. On the other hand, evidence from studies looking at reading instruction and English language learners suggests that instruction with a basic skills focus does not work for this population of learners (Flores, Rueda, & Porter, 1986; Goldman & Rueda, 1988; López-Reyna, 1996; Rueda & Mehan, 1986; Ruiz, 1995a, 1995b, 1999; Ruiz & Figueroa, 1995; Ruiz, Rueda, Figueroa, & Boothroyd, 1995; Trueba, 1987; Viera, 1986; Willig & Swedo, 1987).

Thus, the fundamental question becomes: For an English language learner who is not learning in the general education classroom, what is an enriched educational context, particularly where there is no primary language instruction? Where can a diagnostician observe such a student?

Several recent publications, based on empirical work, concur on what generally promotes academic learning among second language learners (Graves, Valles, & Rueda, 2000; Gutiérrez & Stone, 1997; Ruiz & Figueroa, 1995; Tharp, 1997). First, English language learners learn best when learning activities build on their home language and culture. The principle of constructivism, of using what the child already knows in order to assimilate new knowledge, undergirds every major statement about English language learners' growth in academic achievement. Second, English language learning occurs best in an educational context that is rich in language input, multiple forms of literacy, various types of organizational structures (e.g., cooperative, dyad, and individual), and multiple forms of instructional strategies (e.g., Socratic, interactive, and lecture).

Tharp (1997) has distilled recent thinking in the field of English language teaching and learning into five pedagogical principles. Synthesizing the work of many researchers at the National Center for Research on Education, Diversity and Excellence (CREDE) at the University of California at Santa Cruz, Tharp's principles represent one of the most robust, empirically based statements on how to create enriched, effective instructional contexts for learners experiencing academic difficulties.

Learning is facilitated under the following conditions:

- An expert and a novice work jointly on a task (Moll, 1990; Rogoff, 1991; Tharp & Gallimore, 1988).
- Academic language development is an integral part of instructional activity and builds on the learner's strengths in the native language (Tharp, 1997, p. 7).
- Instruction and curriculum build on the experiences and skills of home and community (Au & Jordan, 1981; Erickson & Mohatt, 1982; Moll, 1992; Wyatt, 1978-1979).
- School work is cognitively complex and challenging, similar to what takes place in classes for the gifted rather than focused on "rote, repetitive, detail-level skills" (Tharp, 1997, p. 8).
- Teacher-student dialogues, "the process of questioning and sharing ideas," are a primary vehicle for learning both basic skills and higher order thinking. Like parents in natural teaching, teachers who use this approach assume that the student has something to say beyond the known answers in the head of the adult. The adult listens carefully, makes guesses about the student's intended meaning, and adjusts responses to assist the student's efforts (Tharp, 1997, p. 8).

While this new awareness of the social, contextual nature of classroom learning has yet to be fully appreciated in special education, it is influencing other educational areas, as behaviorist and reductionist models of how children learn and how they should be assessed are giving way to models that are more contextualized and constructivist. The National Research Council, for example, has made this new understanding of learning and assessment a cornerstone for reforming the National Assessment for Educational Progress (NAEP) (Pellegrino, Jones, & Mitchell, 1999).

Testers who work with English language learners need to understand this development even though it may seem to betray traditional educational psychology. They need to understand that the enriched classroom context may well be the only avenue for determining educational needs and appropriate interventions for English language learners. They need to know that it is more important to understand how instructional context can facilitate academic achievement than it is to speculate about IQ, the possibility of a disability, or the always-hypothetical linkages between a disability and a special educational treatment. Indeed, the school psychologist may have to conclude that knowing how an English language learner processes lessons, instruction, and information may well be impossible in the traditional paradigm because of the multiple linguistic, developmental, and contextual interactions that can take place at any one time.

If learning is a function of context, the diagnostician needs to be able to do two things: Help teachers create reliable and replicable optimal learning contexts, and collect student work products that show how a child is learning over a long period of time and how much of what is learned is generalized and retained. The best artifacts in this regard are the written work products produced in a classroom that builds on a child's background and prior experience and that provides a rich, instructional context (Flores, Rueda, & Porter, 1986; Goldman & Rueda, 1988; Graves, Valles, & Rueda, 2000; Gutiérrez & Stone, 1997; López-Reyna, 1996). In such contexts and with such work products, it may even be feasible to work with an interpreter or translator in an effective and valid manner.

Improving the Referral and Placement Processes

In 1975, the Education for All Handicapped Children Act (Public Law 94-142), renamed the Individuals With Disabilities Education Act in 1990, opened the doors to public education for children with disabilities. For special education assessment personnel, however, this landmark legislation had profound implication for their professional work. They were made into testers, sometimes almost exclusively.

Diagnosticians need to broaden their professional roles. It may not be possible to revolutionize the special education system as it currently exists, but it may be possible to reduce its demands for traditional diagnostic testing. The answer may lie in what happens before the special education referral.

In the Elk Grove Unified School District, just south of Sacramento, California, Cavanaugh (1999) has developed a unique organizational model that offers promise for the field of special education. Motivated in part by the increasing numbers of children who were receiving special education services (and who in turn made greater demands on the resources of the school district), Cavanaugh set out to see if he could reduce these numbers without ignoring student needs. After obtaining special permission from the state to use special education funds, he invited schools in his district to participate in an experiment. With the approval of school faculty, he set up learning centers in each participating school. Teachers could send their underachieving students to this learning center for substantial periods of time during the school day and the school semester in order to receive intensive help. This type of placement was not a referral to special education, and the help was not predicated on the existence of a disability. Over a period of 7 years, Cavanaugh succeeded in reducing the special education enrollment in the school district by 44%. Currently, only .6% of the pupils in the school district are assessed for special education in the traditional manner. The students who attend the learning centers make significant academic progress each year.

Cavanaugh's program was not developed for English language learners and does not incorporate the principles that Tharp (1997) and his colleagues prescribe. Nonetheless, the program's impact on the numbers of students being referred for special education is noteworthy. Academic help is immediate. Assessments occur in the context of intensive school and community interventions. Lack of progress over the long term becomes the primary basis for a subsequent referral to special education. Such a referral, after intensive observation of and work with the student, becomes the basis for an individualized educational plan (IEP) that is not the product of a medical model diagnosis but rather of a long-term educational intervention.

If Cavanaugh's model, called *Neverstreaming,* can be infused with the educational features discussed here for English language learners, assessment personnel may be able to carry out the longitudinal observational work that will enable them to disentangle and understand cultural, linguistic, socioeconomic, and other factors that influence student learning and to use this information to design intervention plans. As a member of the learning center and of the regional teams that provide auxiliary social services, the school diagnostician can define a new professional role that focuses on working closely and collaboratively with the students, their families, and their teachers. For English language learners in a Neverstreaming learning center, the problems associated with traditional assessment practices may be substantially diminished if not eliminated altogether.

Conclusion

Special education assessment personnel need to explore new avenues for working with children with unique cultural and linguistic characteristics. A program such as Neverstreaming (Cavanaugh, 1999) that can bypass the traditional referral, assessment, and placement process may not be the answer for every location, diagnostician, or student. However, the body of available research on testing English language learners, together with extensive policy and regulatory publications (American Educational Research Association, 1999; U. S. Department of Education, 2000), argues for a shift from a traditional assessment model to one that observes students in enriched and effective instructional contexts.

Considerations in the Assessment of English Language Learners Referred to Special Education

Alba A. Ortiz, *University of Texas at Austin*
James R. Yates, *University of Texas at Austin*

The disproportionate representation of English language learners in special education reflects a general lack of understanding in our school systems of the influence of linguistic, cultural, and socioeconomic differences on student learning (García & Ortiz, 1988; Ortiz & Yates, 2001). Limited English proficiency is often misinterpreted as a disability, while a disability is sometimes misinterpreted as limited English proficiency. In the first case, a student who does not need special education receives it, and in the second case, a student who needs special education does not receive it. In neither case does the student receive what he or she needs.

Disproportionate representation is also the result of school policies and procedures that fail to (a) guide teachers in making referral decisions,

(b) ensure that assessments are nondiscriminatory, (c) help school personnel interpret assessment outcomes, and (d) rule out school-related causes of failure such as inappropriate instruction.

Assessments often fail to produce the data needed to determine whether an English language learner has a disability. Research on Hispanic students with learning disabilities (Ortiz et al., 1985) and communication disorders (Ortiz, García, Wheeler, & Maldonado-Colón, 1986) showed that few students were tested in Spanish, and when they were, adaptations of standardized assessments—such as those that had been translated from English to Spanish—were common. Because the adapted instruments and procedures used were neither valid nor reliable, it was not possible to tell whether students had learning disabilities. Thus, basing eligibility decisions on these data was inappropriate.

Even in school districts where bilingual assessment personnel are available, identifying disabilities among English language learners is a complex task (Ortiz & Graves, 2001). Few instruments are available in languages other than English. When they are available, they often have poor psychometric properties, and assessment personnel often have little or no training in assessing second language learners. Most assessment personnel have been taught to assess in English and have not been trained to understand the interaction of disabilities and linguistic, cultural, and other student characteristics.

The long-standing history of the disproportionate representation of students from culturally and linguistically diverse backgrounds in special education has led Figueroa (this volume) to conclude that the current special education assessment system cannot be fixed; it must be reformed. He calls for a shift from a traditional psychometric model to a model in which the child's performance in a learning environment forms the basis for decisions about special education eligibility. Baca (this volume) agrees that reform is needed but notes that "changing federal laws will take time. In the meantime, assessment personnel will continue to rely on existing practices, making it important to minimize biases inherent in traditional processes" (p. 185).

This chapter discusses a framework for planning and conducting special education evaluations of English language learners, interpreting results, establishing eligibility and educational needs, and planning individualized education programs.

The framework assumes that prevention and early intervention efforts such as those suggested by Ortiz (this volume) have been carried out and that the student is still experiencing difficulties, suggesting the need for special education support. The decision to conduct a full and individual initial evaluation to determine whether the student qualifies for special education is made only after the following conditions have been met:

- The teacher uses instructional strategies known to be effective for English language learners.
- Neither clinical teaching nor interventions designed by teacher support teams have resolved learning difficulties.
- Other general education alternatives also have also proven unsuccessful.

If these conditions have been met, it is likely that the student who continues to struggle, despite extensive efforts to individualize instruction, has disabilities (García & Ortiz, 1988; Ortiz, 1997; Ortiz & Wilkinson, 1991). If data indicate that as a group English language learners have limited academic success, the school climate should be evaluated and modifications made to improve the achievement of these students.

Using Professional Assessment Personnel

School systems should make every effort to use qualified professionals in assessments of English language learners. As Ortiz and Yates (2001) suggest, assessment personnel should have a good understanding of first and second language acquisition theory, effective instructional practices for English language learners with disabilities, and the influence of such factors as culture and socioeconomic status on student performance. With respect to assessment, they need to know how to do the following:

- Conduct assessments in the native language and in English, using English as a second language (ESL) approaches.
- Involve parents and family members in referral and assessment processes.
- Adapt standardized assessment instruments and procedures and develop alternatives to traditional procedures.
- Interpret assessment outcomes.
- Apply special education eligibility criteria to native language and English language performance on assessment measures.
- Maintain high ethical standards (e.g., by respecting confidentiality).

Assessment personnel should assess their own knowledge, skills, and values (Heur, 1997) to determine whether they have the background to work effectively with English language learners. If they conclude that they do not have the necessary skills and values, they should refer the students to other evaluators (Leung, 1996). By doing so, they will minimize the possibility that their own perceptions of the child, or the child's racial and ethnic group, will negatively affect the assessment.

If a school district does not have bilingual evaluators, every effort must be made to contract the services of such personnel. To facilitate this, districts and state education agencies should maintain a list of bilingual evaluators who are qualified to assess in languages other than English. If assessment personnel are unable to obtain the services of bilingual evaluators, they should seek the assistance of bilingual professionals from within the school or district (e.g., bilingual education teachers, general education teachers who are bilingual, and bilingual counselors). If these efforts are unsuccessful, the school should seek the services of bilingual professionals in the local community. It is not unusual, for example, to find bilingual teachers in the community who are working outside their profession because they are not certified to teach in the United States. Special licensing or certification is not required to administer many of the assessments used for special education eligibility (e.g., vocabulary, achievement, and language dominance and proficiency assessments). The advantage of having bilingual education teachers participate in special education assessments is that, in addition to their bilingualism, they understand native and English language development and cultural influences. They are also familiar with bilingual education and ESL curricula, instructional strategies, and approaches. This knowledge is crucial not only in determining student eligibility but also in planning instruction for English language learners with disabilities. If bilingual professionals are not available, then using bilingual nonprofessionals (e.g., paraprofessionals) in the school district or bilingual nonprofessionals from the community should be the next option considered.

Both professionals and nonprofessionals alike must understand the purpose of the comprehensive evaluation of students for eligibility for special education services. Bilingual individuals who assist monolingual examiners should also receive training in the principles of assessment as well as in different aspects of test administration: how to administer specific instruments, how to arrange the testing setting and materials, how to interact appropriately with examinees, how to record responses and information that may be helpful in interpreting responses, and how to protect the security of test materials (Kayser, 1995; Muñoz-Sandoval, Cummins, Alvarado, & Rueff, 1998). These assistants must practice the administration and scoring of the assessments under the supervision of assessment personnel. If the supervisory staff are monolingual, they will need the assistance of bilingual professionals who can evaluate the skills of assistant examiners. Before being allowed to assess students, assistants must demonstrate that they can do so accurately and reliably. This step is crucial when appraisal personnel are themselves not bilingual.

The use of interpreters in student assessment is a controversial topic (Figueroa, this volume; Valdés & Figueroa, 1994). However, decisions about special education eligibility that are based on some knowledge of how students function in their native language is preferable to decisions based entirely on their performance in English. The problem is not so much the use of interpreters but rather the use of untrained interpreters who are not proficient in the student's native language— an all-too-frequent practice that assessment reports do not acknowledge. It is unacceptable for an assessor to ask the school secretary, the custodian, or an older sibling to provide on-the-spot interpretation when conducting an assessment.

Individuals who serve as interpreters must have native-like proficiency in the student's dominant language. Not only must they have the skills to administer assessments in the student's native language, but they must also be proficient enough to provide on-the-spot interpretation of complex information relating to the special education processes. It cannot be assumed that anyone who is bilingual has the language proficiency to interpret effectively (Kayser, 1995). An interpreter's language proficiency should be assessed as is required for certification as a bilingual education teacher.

Assessment personnel must be trained to use interpreters effectively. Kayser (1995) recommends that the assessor meet with the interpreter before an evaluation to review the general purpose of the session, to share background information about the child and the family, and to give the interpreter an opportunity to review assessment materials. While the interpreter meets with the family or administers assessments, the assessor should observe these interactions. Even an assessor who is not bilingual can observe the interactions and record impressions about body language, patterns of reinforcement, cueing, and the amount of talk. The assessor and the interpreter then meet to discuss the interview and the results of the assessment, the interpreter's impressions of these, and the assessor's observations. Training interpreters, and using this briefing-assessment-debriefing process, increases the likelihood that information generated with the assistance of the interpreter is accurate and useful.

Planning and Administering the Assessment

Assessment personnel should begin by reviewing existing data. These include teacher referral data, information generated by the clinical teaching and Teacher Assistance Team (Chalfant & Pysh, 1989) processes, and results of district- and state-level tests. This review should generate questions that move the assessment beyond the routine administration of tests to a full and individual evaluation.

A tremendous amount of information is gathered over the course of an English language learner's school career. This information includes annual language dominance assessment results, decisions made by bilingual education and ESL committees, language(s) of instruction at each grade level, special education recommendations, and individualized educational plans (IEPs). However, this information is recorded on many different forms, which are kept in many different files and locations. Consequently, neither bilingual education nor special education committees typically have the benefit of all of the available data when they make decisions about eligibility and program placements or when they develop instructional plans or programs (Ortiz & Graves, 2001). District staff should develop forms and technology that allow student data to be captured in one place. Easy access to this information is crucial for assessment personnel.

The Individuals With Disabilities Education Act Amendments (1997) require that assessments be conducted in the child's native language, unless it is clearly not feasible to do so. An important component of the initial review then is to determine the student's language dominance and proficiency. Language *proficiency* refers to a student's skill level in the use of the language (Payan, 1984), while the *dominant* language is the one in which the student shows the greatest level of skill (Mattes & Omark, 1984). A student can be dominant in a language but not proficient in it. If, for example, a student's performance on a language assessment indicates that she is a non-English speaker, and the Spanish score classifies her as a limited Spanish speaker, Spanish would be considered the dominant language (i.e., the language in which she shows greater skill). However, the student is not a proficient Spanish speaker because she demonstrates a low level of skill in that language.

In most states, English language learners are assessed each year using language proficiency instruments such as the *Language Assessment Scales–Oral* (Duncan & De Avila, 1990) or the *IDEA Individual Language Proficiency Test* (Dalton, 1989). If language data are unavailable, or if they are more than 6 months old, the assessor should request that they be updated (Ortiz & García, 1990). If this is not done, it is the assessor's responsibility to assess language dominance and proficiency so that eligibility decisions and instructional planning are informed by current language data. The assessment must demonstrate that the disability is evident in the dominant language or rule out limited English proficiency as the cause of the learning difficulties.

General Guidelines
While it is beyond the scope of this chapter to review standardized instruments that are used in assessing English language learners, some general guidelines are offered, followed by a discussion of assessment of language proficiency, achievement, and intelligence.

Assess in Both Languages
English language learners should be assessed in both the native language and in English. Otherwise, the evaluator may come to the wrong conclusion about the students' language skills. For example, some children understand a language other than English but refuse to speak it for a variety of reasons. Their parents may understand English but not speak it. They interact with their child in their native language, and the child, in turn, responds in English. Because the parents and child understand each other, they communicate successfully, albeit in different languages. Unless the child's native language skills are assessed, the assessor might inaccurately conclude that the child is an English monolingual.

Use Equivalent Instruments and Procedures in the Native Language and in English

Whenever possible, equivalent instruments and procedures should be administered in English and the native language. In this way, assessors will be able to compare what students know in each language, and they will also be able to describe what students know cumulatively. For example, a student who knows 10 vocabulary words in Spanish and 10 different words in English should be credited with knowing 20 vocabulary words. Not to do so underestimates the student's abilities (Muñoz-Sandoval, Cummins, Alvarado, & Rueff, 1998; Ortiz & Yates, 2001). This is not to say that scores from administrations in each language should be added together but rather that patterns of strengths and weakness should reflect all that a student knows and can do, regardless of the language in which the skill is demonstrated.

When Testing Only in English, Establish the Student's Level of English Proficiency

When students are assessed only in English, the special education eligibility decision will hinge on ruling out lack of English proficiency as the root of the problem. In these instances, the assessor must establish the student's functioning level in English. Ideally, before referring the student, the teacher would have established the baseline of what the student knows, provided ESL instruction for a period of time, and documented progress. With appropriate instruction, students without disabilities will demonstrate increased English proficiency. Students with disabilities will struggle despite the interventions. They are the ones who should be referred. If documentation of ESL instruction is unavailable, then the assessor should consider using curriculum-based assessments such as those described on p. 69.

Use Valid and Reliable Instruments

The Individual With Disabilities Acts Amendments (1997) require that tests and other evaluation materials be free of racial or cultural bias, that standardized tests be validated for the purposes for which they are used, and that tests be administered in accordance with the instructions of test publishers. Relying on tests with questionable sampling procedures, cultural specificity, and poor reliability and validity yields incomplete or inappropriate information (Figueroa, this volume; Leung, 1996).

Determine Appropriate Adaptations of Instruments and Procedures

Given the lack of technically sound instruments for English language learners, it is necessary to identify alternative assessments and to determine acceptable adaptations of standardized assessments. Results of standardized tests must be cross-validated with data from other sources (Leung, 1996). For example, results of norm-referenced reading assessments in the native language and English can be compared with those of informal reading inventories in both languages. If the student's performance is low on formal and informal assessments, it is more likely that the student has a disability.

It is important to bear in mind that alternative assessments have many of the same limitations as traditionally used instruments, and they may not provide a comprehensive picture of students' skills and abilities (Damico, 1991; Shinn & Tindal, 1988). For example, translating instruments invalidates them unless the translations are normed. Thus, results from adapted tests or nonstandard administrations of a test cannot be the basis for determining special education eligibility. Test scores derived from inappropriate instruments should not be reported. Instead, data should be used for diagnostic purposes—that is, to pinpoint problem areas and to describe patterns of strengths and weaknesses. Evaluators and other school personnel involved in determining special education eligibility should use these descriptive data, not test scores, to decide whether the student qualifies for special education.

Language Proficiency Assessments

Language assessment data should be current—that is, not more than 6 months old (Ortiz et al., 1985)—and should describe receptive (listening and reading) and expressive (speaking and writing) skills in both the native and the second languages (Ortiz & Kushner, 1997). If current language proficiency data are unavailable, establishing a student's language dominance and proficiency becomes a major component of the comprehensive evaluation.

Traditionally used norm-referenced instruments provide incomplete profiles of students' language skills because they do not assess language in natural communication situations (Damico, 1991). Norm-referenced assessments tend to focus on the sound system and grammar and ignore conversational abilities and academic language proficiency skills (e.g., using language to predict, evaluate, and infer) (Cummins, 1989). Ortiz and García (1990) recommend the use of procedures that assess these other skills as well. These procedures include the following:

- Spontaneous conversation samples to assess how well a student understands and speaks the two languages with different people and in different settings and contexts
- Story-retelling or dictation tasks to assess receptive academic language proficiency and the ability to understand classroom discourse and lesson content
- Storytelling tasks to assess narrative skills and the child's ability to organize information, sequence events, draw conclusions, and evaluate actions
- Cloze tests to assess a student's background knowledge and knowledge of vocabulary and grammatical structures
- Interviews with parents or family members to gain an understanding of language use in the home and community, language preference, and the level of proficiency in the native language

Results of these measures are then compared with the results of standardized language tests. Low performance on both, along with corroboration from parents that they too are concerned about their child's communication skills, suggests the presence of a disability.

In interpreting language information, examiners must bear in mind that language characteristics will be influenced by such factors as social class and the region of the student's home community in the native country. When the language of a group shows regular variations in phonology, vocabulary, and syntax from what is considered to be "standard" or customary use of that language, the group is said to speak a dialect (Fromkin & Rodman, 1988). Too often, dialectal variations are inaccurately considered limited or substandard forms of the standard language. Yet according to Fromkin and Rodman (1988),

> A standard dialect (or prestige dialect) may have social function—to bind people together or to provide a common written form for multidialectal speakers. It is, however, neither more expressive, more logical, more complex, nor more regular than any other dialect. Any judgements, therefore, as to the superiority or inferiority of a particular dialect are social judgements, not linguistic or scientific ones. (pp. 263-264)

Assessment personnel must consider whether the student is using a dialect of the native language so that they do not misdiagnose language varieties as disabilities.

Assessments of Achievement and Intelligence

Poor academic performance is the primary reason for the referral of English language learners to special education (Ortiz et. al, 1985). Moreover, identification of specific disabilities (e.g., learning disabilities as opposed to mental retardation) is based on the relationship between academic achievement and intellectual potential. Accordingly, assessments of achievement and intelligence are critical aspects of the initial evaluation.

Assessment of Achievement

For students who have received bilingual education, academic achievement should be assessed in the native language and in English. When students are assessed in English, the assessor must answer the question, "Does the student have enough English to understand and perform this task?" A student's score on an assessment may be low because the language used in the test is beyond the student's English proficiency level. It is also possible that the student knew an answer to a question but was unable to provide it in English. Achievement results thus must be weighed against the student's English language skills. Assessors should note correct answers even if the language in which the student responded did not match the language of the assessment.

The limitations of language assessment instruments are also limitations of traditionally used achievement tests. It is necessary, then, to supplement norm-referenced instruments with performance-based measures that tell teachers what students can do and what they know, not just how they compare to other students. Cheng (1997) and Feuerstein (1979) recommend a dynamic assessment model that involves assessing performance, teaching to the task, and then testing again to gauge the student's response to the intervention. The assessor analyzes the conditions under which the student learns the task. Because such curriculum-based assessments (Tucker, 1985) are based on the materials being used to teach the student, it is possible to determine what the student knows, what she or he needs to learn, and where in the curriculum the student should begin. Repeated assessments are used to fine-tune instruction and to track progress, providing teachers with portfolios of student work. Portfolios offer a tremendous advantage because they provide a view of achievement over time and in different areas, including language development and academic achievement in the native language and in English (Farr & Trumbull, 1997).

Such approaches to assessment offer several advantages for English language learners (Ortiz & Wilkinson, 1991). Student performance in the native language and in English can be measured. Assessors can compare performance across languages to determine whether deficits are associated with a possible disability or whether they reflect the process of second language acquisition. Furthermore, by assessing skills in both languages, interventions that foster first and second language learning can be developed.

Assessment of Intelligence

We do not yet have technically sound tests of intelligence (IQ) or cognitive skills in languages other than English. Even when racial and ethnic groups are represented in a standardization sample, tests are usually not normed specifically for English language learners. For these students, verbal IQ tests become measures of the student's language proficiency. Assessments of intelligence thus should include nonverbal measures (Holtzman & Wilkinson, 1991).

Although nonverbal intelligence tests are preferred over verbal tests for assessing the intelligence of English language learners, such tests cannot predict how students will perform in classes where success depends on the ability to use language for both social and academic purposes. It is thus important that assessments of intelligence be supplemented with additional information. Holtzman and Wilkinson (1991) suggest that evaluators do the following:

- Insist on pre-referral intervention to take care of the difficulties before a formal assessment has been initiated.
- Evaluate the situation to ensure that the referral does not reflect bias or a lack of knowledge.
- Observe the student in various educational contexts to better understand how different the student's behavior is from that of peers.
- "Calibrate" expectations of student performance—that is, describe the behaviors needed for success in a particular setting and compare the student's current functioning level with those criteria.

Reporting the Results

After the necessary assessments have been administered, evaluators report the data, making sure that the assessments generate enough information to identify students' strengths and weaknesses. As indicated previously, evaluators should report student performance in the native language and in English *in aggregate*. Results should be considered in light of students' school history and progress in the general education curriculum and should corroborate the concerns identified by teachers and parents at the point of referral. If a student has a history of academic difficulties, the referral committee should have documented that these problems were not resolved even though alternative programs and services were provided. Without such evidence, it will be difficult to rule out lack of opportunity as the cause of learning difficulties.

In preparing the evaluation report, the assessor should report all adaptations of instruments and procedures and should describe the nature of bilingual assessments, noting, for example, if an interpreter was used, if instruments were translated on the spot, and if items missed in English were administered in the native language. Scores on formal instruments should not be reported if the norms are not appropriate for the student being assessed or if administrations were nonstandard. Instead, patterns of student strengths and weaknesses should be described and used diagnostically to support eligibility decisions. If performance on the formal and informal measures converge, multidisciplinary teams can be more confident that the student has a disability. If decisions are based only on results of standardized measures, there will be a lingering question as to whether the low performance was a result of the instruments used.

Determining Eligibility

It is the responsibility of a multidisciplinary team to review the results of the assessments and to determine whether a student has a legally defined disability and needs special education services.

Team Membership

By law, the multidisciplinary team is made up of a representative of the school administration, instructional representatives from special education and general education, assessors, the student's parent, and, if appropriate, the student. It is important that the team include representatives who understand the unique considerations in educating English language learners (Ortiz & Yates, 2001). If the student is in a bilingual education program, the teacher(s) will participate in the team meeting. If the student is in an ESL program, the ESL teacher should be invited to participate, along with the child's general education teacher. If the student is participating in an alternative program (e.g., Title I) or is receiving medical services (e.g., from the school nurse), a representative from these programs and services also should be included. If the meeting is conducted in English, a trained interpreter should attend so that parents with limited English can participate meaningfully in team deliberations.

Some states require that a representative from bilingual education or the ESL program serve on the team. By the same token, special educators should serve on special language program committees that determine continued eligibility for bilingual education and ESL services. Members of these committees should receive training so that they understand the purposes of their respective programs, eligibility criteria, federal and state policies governing service delivery, and curricula and instruction.

Team Responsibilities

In reaching their decision that a student is eligible for special education services, team members must provide assurances that the student's problems are not the result of a lack of academic support or of limited English proficiency, cultural differences, or other student characteristics. In providing these assurances, the team should clearly describe and be able to support the data that it used to reach its conclusions. For example, the team cannot rule out limited English proficiency as the source of the difficulty if language assessment results are outdated or if assessments were conducted entirely in English.

Answering questions such as the ones that follow (adapted from Damico, 1991) can help the team rule out factors other than the presence of a disability as the source of difficulties.

- In addition to the general education teacher, have others (e.g., the ESL teacher, remedial program personnel, and parents) noted similar difficulties?

- Does the problem exist across contexts (e.g., in general education and ESL classes, at school, and at home)? For example, if the student acts out in class, do the parents report similar behavior at home?
- Are the problems evident in the student's first language? For example, do native speakers of the student's language have difficulty understanding him or her? Does the student have difficulty following instructions in the native language as well as in English? Has the student not learned to read in the native language, despite effective literacy instruction in that language?
- Is the student's progress in acquiring English significantly different from that of peers who started at about the same level of English language proficiency and have had comparable instruction?
- Is there evidence that difficulties can be explained by cross-cultural differences? For example, a lack of eye contact, which a teacher might interpret as defiance, could be considered appropriate behavior in the child's native culture, or a student's narrative patterns might reflect patterns typical of storytelling in the home culture.
- Are there other variables that could explain the difficulties? Such variables might include inconsistent school attendance or language variations typical of English language learners.
- Is there evidence of extreme test anxiety (as can occur when the child being tested has been in the country for only a short time)?
- Can problematic behaviors be explained by procedural mistakes in the assessment process (e.g., the child's age was calculated incorrectly)?
- Can problematic behaviors be explained by bias in operation before, during, or after the assessment? For example, bias is an issue when the student's teacher refers all English language learners in the classroom for special education, when the instruments used are not normed for English language learners or the adaptations used are inappropriate, and when the assessor's low expectations for student performance influence the administration and interpretation of results.

- Do data show that the student did not respond well to general education interventions? For example, were clinical teaching, support team interventions, and alternative programs unsuccessful in closing achievement gaps?
- Are the assessment results consistent with the concerns of the student's teachers and parents?

If the student's problems cannot be explained by factors such as those above, then the team is in a better position to conclude that the student has a disability.

Team members will sometimes recommend special education placement for failing students even though they do not qualify or problems identified do not mesh with the reasons for referral. Team members may reason that if children are failing in the general education classroom, there is no harm in putting them in special education. Research suggests otherwise, however. Wilkinson and Ortiz (1986) found that after 3 years of special education services, Hispanic students diagnosed with learning disabilities had actually lost ground. Their IQ scores were lower than they had been at entry into special education, while their achievement scores were at essentially the same levels as they had been. This suggests that a label of disability is not in the interest of children who do not clearly meet eligibility criteria. Instead, educators should adapt general education programs and services to the needs of English language learners experiencing academic difficulty and provide alternative support systems in the regular program to ensure their academic success.

The multidisciplinary team has other important responsibilities as well. Members develop the individualized education plan (IEP) and decide the extent to which the student will participate in bilingual education, ESL, and the general education program. They also recommend whether the student will be exempted from district- or statewide assessments of achievement. If the student is to be included, they indicate the language in which the student should be tested and what accommodations must be provided.

Planning Individualized Education Programs and Selecting the Least Restrictive Environment

How the individualized education program (IEP) addresses native language and ESL instruction has significant implications for future assessments, which will focus on student progress as a result of special education intervention. Wilkinson and Ortiz (1986) found that educators planning IEPs for Hispanic students with disabilities were unfamiliar with principles of bilingualism and first and second language acquisition. Of the 203 IEPs examined, only 2% stated that some instruction would be carried out in Spanish; none included ESL goals and objectives. Students' language proficiency had little effect on the design of the special education services provided to them. Yet even the very best special education instruction will be ineffective if it is delivered in a language the student does not understand.

Some educators mistakenly reason that because English language learners with disabilities will have difficulty mastering English skills, the amount and intensity of English instruction should be increased. Because they believe that bilingual instruction will be confusing to students, they remove them from bilingual education programs (Ortiz, 1984). Such reasoning ignores the relationship between native language proficiency and English language acquisition. If students have not acquired the language of their parents, there is little likelihood that they will develop high levels of proficiency in English (Cummins, 1989; Ortiz, 1984). If they have not benefited from instruction in their dominant language, there is no reason to expect that they will make greater progress when instruction is presented in their weaker language.

English language learners do not lose their right to bilingual education or ESL services when they qualify for special education services. On the contrary, students should be educated in the least restrictive environment (Individuals with Disabilities Act Amendments, 1997)—that is, they should have the opportunity to study with peers who are not disabled and to remain in bilingual education, general education, and ESL classes to the maximum extent possible. This guiding principle suggests that English language learners should be provided a continuum of placement alternatives that support native language and English language development at the same time that they address disability-related needs. A focus of the annual review is the appropriateness of the IEP, particularly regarding a student's access to services from general and special education personnel qualified to meet the needs of English language learners with disabilities.

Conducting Annual Reviews

The annual review of students receiving special education services is one of the most important components of the special education process in that it gives multidisciplinary teams the opportunity to identify students who are not making expected progress. The multidisciplinary team is expected to review existing assessment data and to determine whether these data are sufficient to decide whether students continue to be eligible for special education (Individuals with Disabilities Act Amendments, 1997). If there are questions about eligibility or about progress, the committee, or the parent, may request a reevaluation at this time. Even if a reevaluation is not required, since students' English skills may change dramatically over brief periods, frequent reviews of performance may be necessary. Language assessment data should be updated at least annually for English language learners. If students are not progressing adequately, IEPs should be modified and alternative strategies recommended to improve performance.

If students continue to qualify for special education services, IEPs are updated; if students are not progressing adequately, IEPs are modified, and alternative strategies to improve performance are recommended. Students who no longer meet eligibility criteria are withdrawn from special education. It is important to monitor the progress of these students to be sure that their integration into general education on a full-time basis is successful.

Conclusion

As the cultural and linguistic demography of schools continues to change dramatically, education professionals must reform policies, programs, and practices to respond to the needs of English language learners. A comprehensive school reform effort is needed to ensure that English language learners are successful in the general education program and that those who are placed in special education truly have disabilities. While we work to achieve the paradigmatic shift advocated by Figueroa (this volume)—a shift from a model driven by testing to a model that observes students in optimal learning environments—we must work to limit the bias inherent in traditionally used assessment processes. The framework presented in this chapter is a starting point.

translator = Someone

Parent-Professional Collaboration in Culturally Sensitive Assessment

Shernaz B. García, *University of Texas at Austin*

The Individuals With Disabilities Education Act Amendments of 1997 provide the legal basis for involving parents and other family members in the special education process, including the assessment and determination of eligibility for services. Since the Education for All Handicapped Children Act of 1975, legal safeguards for students with disabilities have emphasized the rights of parents to be informed about, to provide consent for, and to attend school meetings related to their children's education. Over time, the legal requirements have evolved from assuming a somewhat passive role for parents to promoting a more informed and active role for them. Yet while the law views families as partners with the school in their children's education, it offers few explicit guidelines to help educators and the families accomplish this partnership.

The lack of guidance is particularly problematic for educators working with learners and families from culturally and linguistically diverse backgrounds. These learners and their families may encounter cultural and linguistic barriers that limit their participation in the education process (Harry, 1992; Harry, Allen, & McLaughlin, 1995; Kalyanpur & Harry, 1999; Lynch & Stein, 1987; Sontag & Schacht, 1994). Philosophically, the notion of a close and equal home-school partnership reinforces the importance of active participation by family members in educational decisions that affect their children. Such a partnership can be a critical step toward improving services for groups that historically have not been served well by the educational system (Artiles & Trent, 1994; Cummins, 1986; García & Dominguez, 1997; Rueda, 1990). However, even the view of parents as equal partners is rooted in the value system of the dominant culture, which assumes that active parent participation in school is a prerequisite for student success (Harry, Rueda, & Kalyanpur, 1999; Vandegrift & Greene, 1992). Students and families from culturally diverse groups may hold different beliefs about the role of parents in education (e.g., Trumbull, Rothstein-Fisch, Greenfield, & Quiroz, 2001). To prevent misunderstanding, miscommunication, and conflicts, educators need to understand the perspectives of the parents and other family members with whom they work.

The extent to which special educators, including school psychologists, educational diagnosticians, and speech and language pathologists, can develop successful home-school partnerships with diverse families depends, then, on their ability to interact with parents in culturally and linguistically responsive ways. The current literature in special education documents the resources and strengths of culturally diverse communities and the failure of the educational system to value these strengths and accommodate this diversity (e.g., Bailey, Skinner, Rodriguez, Gut, & Correa, 1999; Ford, 1995; Harry, 1995; Kalyanpur & Harry, 1999; Kroth & Edge, 1997; Lynch & Hanson, 1998; Méndez Pérez, 1998).

The professional literature also underscores the need to redefine parent involvement (Vandegrift & Greene, 1992), acknowledge diverse cultural beliefs about disability (Harry, 1992, 1995; Lynch & Hanson, 1998; Méndez Pérez, 1998; Romero de Thompson, 1996), and develop a sociocultural framework for interacting with linguistically and culturally diverse families (García, Méndez Pérez, & Ortiz, 2000; Harry, Rueda, & Kalyanpur, 1999). In effect, the literature calls for major changes in the ways that parents are involved in the special education process. As we create new models for assessment and intervention, we must seek more effective ways of communicating with culturally and linguistically diverse families.

This chapter discusses the implications of these new ways of thinking for educators and for families from culturally diverse backgrounds as they interact during the process of assessing children. It begins with a brief review of the legal procedural safeguards and guidelines for parent involvement in the assessment process. It then discusses key concepts and strategies related to the meaningful involvement of families in the assessment process.

Of course, families are diverse not only in language and culture but also in other background characteristics such as race, social class, formal education, and acculturation. How a family participates in the education system will depend on the complex interrelationships of all of these factors. This chapter, however, focuses on only one factor— the impact of culture and language on home-school collaboration during assessment.

Legal Provisions for Involvement of Parents in the Assessment Process

Since their passage in 1997, the Individuals with Disabilities Education Act (IDEA) Amendments have given parents specific rights and responsibilities regarding educational services for children with special needs. These rights are actualized by procedural safeguards that ensure equitable access to special education. While some requirements (e.g., communication in a language understood by the parent) are applicable throughout the special education process, the final regulations for IDEA (IDEA '97 Final Regulations, 1999) also contain requirements specific to the assessment process. The key provisions follow:

- School districts must notify parents of meetings related to their child's assessment for and placement in special education, and of their right to participate in these meetings (§300.501).
- Schools must notify parents in writing of any intent to initiate or change the identification, assessment, or placement of their child. The law specifies the types of information to be included in the notice. School districts must make sure that parents understand the content and language of the notice (§300.503(c)).
- Schools must provide parents a copy of the procedural safeguards, which include provisions related to evaluation, eligibility, and placement (§300.504).
- Parents must provide *informed* consent for the referral, evaluation, and placement of their child in special education (§300.505).
- Parents have the right to review all records related to evaluation, eligibility, and placement (§300.501).
- The assessment process should include evaluations and information provided by the parents (§300.532(b)).
- Evaluation data reviewed by school district personnel must include any evaluations and information provided by the parent (§300.533(a)(2)).
- If parents disagree with the evaluation conducted by the district, they have the right to request an independent evaluation at no cost to them (§300.502(b)(1)).
- Decisions about eligibility and placement must be made with parental input. This means that parents must participate in any group that makes decisions about educational placements, and that school districts are responsible for ensuring that parents understand and are able to participate in such meetings. For parents whose native language is other than English, interpreters must be provided (§300.501; §300.535).
- A copy of the evaluation report and documentation determining disability must be provided to the parents (§300.534(a)).

Implications for Home-School Collaboration

Although IDEA is a legal document, it reflects specific sociocultural assumptions, values, and beliefs about the nature of disability, the role of professionals and parents, and the intended outcomes of educational programs and services for children and youth with disabilities (Kalyanpur & Harry, 1999). In their analysis of the cultural foundations of IDEA's legal principles, Kalyanpur and Harry noted the interactions between societal core values, education, and social policy: Special education programs and services in the United States have been shaped by cultural notions of equity, choice, and individualism. Kalyanpur and Harry also observed that families whose worldviews differ from those of the mainstream culture are likely to experience cultural discomfort as they attempt to participate in their children's education.

Attention to the cultural underpinnings of the law is relatively recent in special education, particularly as the law is applied to culturally and linguistically diverse communities. Examining the legal provisions from a cross-cultural perspective begins with the recognition that *both* schools and families are influenced by their cultural contexts. This approach emphasizes the need to go beyond a focus on the family's cultural and linguistic characteristics and to identify the underlying personal, professional, legal, and organizational values and beliefs that guide school personnel in evaluating students. This section examines the legal provisions of IDEA from a sociocultural perspective and discusses implications for families and for the professionals who work with them.

Defining *Parent*

IDEA's definition of the term *parent* is broad. It includes the natural or adoptive parent of the child, a legal guardian, a surrogate parent, or "a person who is acting in the place of a parent (such as a grandparent or stepparent with whom the child lives, or a person who is legally responsible for the child's welfare)" (§300.20). Because it is broad, the definition accommodates cultural variations in family structure and in roles and responsibilities related to child rearing and guardianship. However, the primary focus, understandably, is still on the student's legal guardian, who, in all likelihood, will continue to be the family's representative in all aspects of the process.

When working with students and families from diverse cultural backgrounds, however, it is important to realize that the customary definition of parent may need to be broadened to include extended family members, as well as others, such as godparents, to reflect the family's kinship system. For some students, another family member (e.g., a grandparent, aunt, or godparent) who has primary child rearing responsibilities may be able to provide more detailed information about the child than the parent. For example, he or she might have important information about the child's daily routine and medical history.

Assessment staff need to have some understanding of who does what in a family: Roles for decision making may be defined by cultural norms based on gender, age, or kinship, so that the parent who attends school meetings may be reluctant to make any decisions without consulting other family members (e.g., spouse or family elders). In these situations, the presence of the legal guardian at meetings may not be sufficient; the decision making process is more likely to go smoothly if the other family members are involved, directly or indirectly.

Informing Parents of Their Legal Rights and Responsibilities

Parents' understanding of their rights and responsibilities is central to their ability to participate meaningfully in the assessment process. Thus, IDEA mandates that parents be provided a copy of the procedural safeguards in a language that they understand. This requirement, however, does not ensure that the safeguards are clear to parents and are carried out. Meaningful family participation also depends on two other factors: the cultural comfort zone of families and the cross-cultural skills of school professionals.

Cultural Comfort Zone of Families

It is important that special educators and other professionals recognize that some families may not be comfortable with the level and types of participation expected of them. If family members seem to be aware of the procedural safeguards, but their interactions with the school do not appear to be consistent with this knowledge, it is possible that they are experiencing some degree of discomfort or that they are operating from very different assumptions about the educational process and their role in it. For example, the expectation that parents have the right to disagree with school personnel may conflict with the belief that group harmony takes precedence over individual rights (Hofstede, 1991), leading parents to be silent during meetings or even to give consent despite their concerns. Some family members may also defer to educators in the belief that "the teacher knows best," reflecting cultural assumptions about the authority and expertise of school personnel to make educational decisions about their children (Hofstede, 1991). School personnel also need to understand that in some instances what appears to be agreement may not be agreement at all: In some cultures, nodding one's head means only that one has understood what was said and does not signify approval or consent. This is an important distinction when decisions are being made about the existence of a disability, interpretation of assessment data, or placement in special education.

Cross-Cultural Skills of Professionals

Given the lower rates of involvement in the special education process among families from culturally and linguistically diverse backgrounds, and the legal and educational emphasis on active participation of family members, professionals are often expected to take an active role in promoting the participation that the law requires. To do so, they must examine their own cultural values as well as those of the family; consider how these two sets of values may be different; and explore how the school can acknowledge, respect, and accommodate the value system of the family (Kalyanpur & Harry, 1999).

The process, then, begins with cultural self-awareness and a recognition of the cultural roots of schooling and educational laws. Only then can educators understand the cultural influences on their own behaviors, values, and beliefs, as well as those reflected in educational practices, including assessment. In addition, professionals must possess knowledge of cultural differences and similarities, so that they can accurately interpret behaviors, understand the underlying values reflected in conversations with parents, and respond in ways that promote successful intercultural communication (Gudykunst & Kim, 1997; Lynch & Hanson, 1998). Professionals who can interact with families in ways that preserve the families' legal rights and responsibilities help create a climate of trust and foster the family's ability to make choices and decisions that are in their best interests. These choices may not always match the expectations of the school. In such instances, respect for the family's cultural traditions can be demonstrated through a willingness to work within the comfort zone of family members.

Obtaining Informed Consent

IDEA guidelines spell out in some detail what is meant by informed parental consent. It means that information must be provided in the parents' native language, if necessary; that it must be complete; that parents must understand the actions being proposed; and that they must consent in writing. The guidelines also acknowledge that some parents may need help to understand the information they have received. Therefore, school notices must include information about resources available to help parents understand the information and services available to them.

The IDEA requirement that parental consent be informed is a significant step toward ensuring that parents actually understand educational information about their children and can participate meaningfully in decisions. Because students from culturally diverse backgrounds continue to be over- and underrepresented in some categories of special education (Artiles & Ortiz, this volume; Artiles & Trent, 1994; Office of Civil Rights, 1997), this consent is a particularly important safeguard.

Although the IDEA provisions are sensitive to the needs of parents who cannot read English or any other language, it is interesting to note that parents are still required to provide *written* consent. This is likely to create difficulties for parents who are not literate in their native language or in English, or whose native language does not have a written code.

While the guidelines address the need for parents to understand the language and content of any information they receive, less attention is paid to cultural values and beliefs that might influence their ability and willingness to give informed consent, even when they fully understand the information they have received. For example, the family's view of disability—whether it exists and how the school should respond—can differ fundamentally from that of school personnel (Harry, 1992; Méndez Pérez, 1998). Families may also differ from school personnel in their assumptions about the roles of teachers and parents in education and in their own expertise in making educational decisions.

Finally, school personnel need to pay attention to the different roles and decision-making responsibilities of different family members. As noted earlier, it may not be enough to inform only the parent (or legal guardian). Others may also need to be informed, and in languages that they understand; thus, the language preference of the parent is only one consideration in determining the most appropriate language(s) and method(s) of communication with the family. Though efforts to include other family members in the process may exceed legal requirements, such efforts demonstrate the school's respect for cultural and linguistic diversity and its sincere desire to accommodate the needs of *all* families in the assessment process.

Gathering Evaluation Information

A central assumption behind assessment is that it should not only accurately diagnose a disability, but it should also support instructional planning (Leung, 1996). An important part of the assessment process is gathering sociological information about the family. Given the extreme shortage of qualified bilingual/bicultural examiners, the assumption that assessment personnel can make informed judgments about the types and sources of information needed for culturally and linguistically diverse groups of students becomes problematic. A preferred approach would be to view family members not simply as sources of data but also as cultural informants (Lynch & Hanson, 1998) and as partners in the process who can help determine what information is needed and how to obtain it. This approach is more likely to work because it is sensitive to the family's beliefs regarding what information is important and how much of it can be shared with school personnel without loss of family honor.

For families to contribute productively to culturally sensitive assessment, school staff need to consider the following factors: the nature of the family's involvement, cultural considerations during data gathering, and the types of data to be gathered.

The Nature of the Family's Involvement

When culturally diverse families are actively involved in gathering assessment information, their contributions provide valuable data about the student's functioning outside of school. Comparisons with school-based data gathered by school personnel can then be helpful in identifying consistencies as well as inconsistencies in academic performance and behavior, and in validating (or challenging) the existence of an academic or behavioral difficulty (García & Ortiz, 1988). Family members should also be involved in determining the types of information to be gathered and in interpreting this information. Their contributions can be very helpful in distinguishing linguistic and cultural differences from disabilities (Baca, de Valenzuela, & García, 1996; Leung, 1996; Ortiz & García, 1990).

A more active role for parents as partners in data collection and interpretation is based on several assumptions: The school and family can devise a mutually agreeable plan for sharing roles and responsibilities; family members will not be asked to perform tasks or assume roles that are beyond their skills and preferences; and both parties will learn from the experience—that is, professionals will value the "funds of knowledge" within each family (Moll, Amanti, Neff, & González, 1992), and parents will have opportunities to acquire the information and skills that they need to fulfill their roles, through guided participation from school personnel (García, Méndez Pérez, & Ortiz, 2000).

Cultural Considerations in Gathering Assessment Data

As parents become more actively involved in gathering information, school personnel will encounter unfamiliar cultural patterns of communication and interaction. These patterns, if misunderstood, increase the likelihood of cultural clashes, which result when "behaviors considered proper and socially skilled in one culture are considered improper or even inappropriate in the other" (Brislin, 1993, p. 10). A few examples of cultural norms that may influence data collection follow.

As assessment personnel begin to gather assessment data, family members may express culturally based views about health, illness, and disability, and these views may differ from those of the school and assessment team. These beliefs are likely to influence the family's interpretation of assessment data, as well as their willingness to initiate medical treatment or an educational intervention related to their child's condition (Hanson, Lynch, & Wayman, 1990). As the assessment team considers what data are needed, norms associated with what is public and what is private (Gudykunst & Ting-Toomey, 1988) may lead to parental reluctance to disclose certain types of information or details that are routinely gathered during assessment but considered private in the family's culture. Similarly, interactions between parents and professionals will be influenced by their respective assumptions about power and authority (Hofstede, 1991). For example, family members may defer to the professionals and have different expectations about who should interact with whom based on age, gender, social status, and the authority of the participants. Norms related to saving face (Gudykunst & Ting-Toomey, 1988) may make some parents reluctant to openly disagree with educators in an effort to spare them embarrassment. Finally, cultural norms may shape family responses to conflict and strategies for its resolution (Gudykunst & Kim, 1997). Family members may ignore a conflict to preserve group harmony, involve a third-party mediator, or confront a disagreement directly.

In addition to cultural norms and value systems that may create conflict, a family's past experience with racism, discrimination, and oppression may affect their perception of the educational system (Ogbu, 1994). Some
parents may have had negative school experiences, which are likely to influence their expectations about the purpose and outcome of the assessment
process as well as their responses to school personnel (Vandegrift &
Greene, 1992). As a result of their past experiences, some parents may
not trust educators, perceiving them to be representatives of a system
that has not provided their community equitable access to educational, economic, or political opportunities (Ogbu, 1994; Parette &
Petch-Hogan, 2000).

Types of Data Gathered

Assessment personnel need accurate cultural and linguistic information
about different areas of students' lives. Information is needed regarding the student's sociological background, developmental and medical
history, language use and development, and social and emotional
functioning. Such information enables assessment staff to make
informed decisions about the language(s) of testing, types of information to be considered in diagnosing a disability, use of culturally and
linguistically relevant strategies for data collection, and interpretation
of the evaluation data.

The sociological background information will give the school knowledge about the student's home life—family child-rearing practices;
family structure; levels of acculturation; languages; and beliefs about
intelligence, disability, and education (García & Dominguez, 1997).
For example, if the family's perceptions about the student do not
match those of educators, assessment personnel need to determine
the cultural bases (if any) for these differences. This information can
help special educators interpret assessment data, validate learning difficulties, and determine culturally sensitive strategies for involving families in the evaluation process.

Information about the student's developmental and medical history may be intertwined with information about the family's child rearing practices or the child's life experiences. As parents share this information, assessment personnel are likely to encounter a variety of responses to their questions about the child's difficulties. Depending on the symptoms involved, the family may not share educators' concerns about the condition, or they may turn to traditional treatments rather than to modern medicine. These decisions are also likely to be based on culturally different assumptions about the causes of the condition as well as about health and healing. They may also involve a different set of beliefs about the link between mind and body and appropriate sources of medical information and forms of medical practice (Hanson, Lynch, & Wayman, 1990).

It is equally important to take into account individual levels of acculturation and family practices. For example, Latino parents in recent studies (Bailey et al., 1999; Méndez Pérez, 1998) did not seem to hold traditional theories about their children's disabilities nor did they seek traditional remedies as the primary treatment for their children with special needs. Failure to consider an individual family's belief system and health practices may cause school professionals to misinterpret data, make decisions based on incomplete information, and inadvertently create barriers to the involvement of the family in the assessment process.

In the area of language use and development, parents and other family members can help construct a language profile for the student (Ortiz & García, 1990), particularly regarding languages used in the home and community. When the languages or dialects used in these settings are different from those of the school, this information will help to determine the student's proficiency in both the native language and English. This information in turn may help the school determine the most appropriate language(s) for assessment and provide valuable contextual data to interpret the student's performance on measures of intelligence and achievement. Given sociocultural variations in language use (Gudykunst & Kim, 1997; Heath, 1982,

1986), information should also be gathered about the family's communication styles, literacy practices, and perceptions about language development.

The family can also provide valuable information about the student's social and emotional functioning, helping assessment staff understand how culturally based child rearing beliefs and practices have influenced the student's social skill development. Discussions with parents will also help staff understand which behaviors are acceptable in what contexts. This information not only yields a more accurate diagnosis of an emotional or behavioral disorder but can also contribute to the development of a social skills curriculum for learners who need guidance in this area (Cartledge & Milburn, 1996). If the family shares concerns about their child's social and emotional difficulties, their perceptions about the health care system and cultural beliefs about mental health should be taken into account. These perceptions and beliefs will influence their willingness to seek support from formal sources, such as counselors, psychologists, and doctors, in addition to other, more informal or community-based groups, such as churches, extended family, and friends (Romero de Thompson, 1996).

Determining Eligibility and Educational Needs

Determining a child's eligibility for special education is a significant step because of its far-reaching educational consequences. The 1997 amendments to IDEA gave parents a much more active role in determining eligibility for special education services as well as in identifying educational needs. The amendments are designed to help placement committees distinguish cultural and linguistic differences from disability and thus to safeguard against inappropriate diagnosis and evaluation. But the amendments implicitly assume that the new roles will be within the comfort zone of family members and that professionals possess the cross-cultural skills to interact successfully with them. These assumptions ignore the sociocultural and linguistic disparities that have traditionally limited parent participation in the process.

Determining Eligibility

Cultural beliefs about disability and parental authority are likely to guide parents during this stage of the process. For instance, parents may not always agree that there is a disability, even though the evaluation data indicate one. They may have difficulty understanding the rationale for placement in special education if their views of normality and disability are different from those embedded in law (Harry, 1992), or if their expectations are guided by a different set of developmental norms—regarding, for example, cognition, language and communication, motor development, and self-help skills. In such instances, discussion should first focus on ensuring that parents have the right information regarding eligibility criteria, the child's level of functioning, and the potential impact of the disability on future educational progress. If this information does not seem to convince the parents of the need for special services, it may be more productive for team members to demonstrate the educational benefits of the services and the link between the proposed services and educational goals that are important to the family. The intent here is not to manipulate the family into agreeing to the services, but rather to find common ground on which to establish an appropriate educational program (García, Méndez Pérez, & Ortiz, 2000).

Even behind this approach is a cultural assumption—that family members are comfortable with dissent, particularly in the more public forum of a team meeting. When families find dissent uncomfortable, the failure to understand and accept the cultural bases for their interactions may lead to a misinterpretation of the family's response as denial, ignorance, lack of cooperation, or lack of assertiveness. If, on the other hand, professionals are knowledgeable about cultural variations in communication and conflict resolution, and are attuned to verbal as well as nonverbal cues from parents about their feelings and thoughts, it is more likely that these differences will be resolved in a climate of cultural reciprocity.

Determining Educational Needs

To accurately determine a child's educational needs, families and school personnel must work together from a foundation of shared educational goals for the student. In contrast to special education services for preschool children, which necessarily focus on the parent, services for the public school student are more student centered (Hanson, Lynch, & Wayman, 1990). This shift in focus from parent to child may inadvertently subordinate the family's educational goals to those of the school curriculum, creating conflicts with the family regarding what is important for children to learn (García & Malkin, 1993).

An accurate evaluation of the student's educational needs is important when diagnosing a disability, developing an individualized education plan (IEP), and monitoring progress. Legal guidelines clearly require evidence of educational need in order to qualify students with disabilities for special education. This documentation should bring together the academic or behavioral goals, classroom observations, assessment data, and judgments of both school personnel and family members regarding the student's educational needs. Culturally sensitive assessment practices include efforts by educators to elicit and understand the family's views on education and to address these views during discussions about eligibility, IEP development, and reviews of student progress.

Conclusion

Involving families from diverse linguistic and cultural groups in assessment for special education services helps to ensure that programs and services for children are appropriate and meet the intent of the law. Such an approach requires ongoing collaboration among educators, families, and the larger community. A sociocultural perspective of family involvement places assessment in the context of culture, creating an environment of mutual respect that allows schools and families to work together (García, Méndez Pérez, & Ortiz, 2000). If we are to achieve meaningful partnerships with diverse families, we must be able to learn from them and to respect and value their contributions to the assessment process, no matter how different they may be from our own professionally based assumptions about parent involvement. Professionals who adopt a sociocultural framework grounded in the principle of cultural reciprocity (Kalyanpur & Harry, 1999) are more likely to understand that our system's legal and educational expectations for family involvement may not always match the interests, abilities, and needs of culturally diverse families. While this can be true for any family, it is particularly relevant for families who do not share the views of mainstream society. A sociocultural approach provides the foundation for parents and professionals to come together to achieve a mutually desired goal: the provision of appropriate educational services based on principles of equity and self-determination.

Instruction

Culturally and Linguistically Responsive Instructional Planning

Nancy Cloud, *Rhode Island College*

In terms of teacher effectiveness and student success, there is probably no more important step in teaching than instructional planning. Required by the 1997 Individuals With Disabilities Education Act Amendments, instructional planning is carried out through the individualized education plan (IEP). Instructional planning is critically important to the learning process because it is how teachers link learning theory with action (Schön, 1983; Wein, 1995). Planning "forces teachers to identify what they will teach and how" (Polloway, Patton & Serna, 2001, p. 37). Based on students' strengths and needs, as identified by teachers, parents, and students themselves, instructional planning is how teachers actualize their students' IEPs, using a continuous process of assessment, reflection, and action.

In the case of English language learners with special education needs, it is through planning that teachers ensure well-integrated instruction that simultaneously focuses on students' cultural characteristics,[1]

[1]The term *cultural characteristics* refers to students' culturally determined beliefs, norms, values, customs, and patterns of thought and behavior. These are continuously influenced by a child's primary cultural group membership, family norms, and wider societal influences. While ethnicity and nationality can affect a child's individual cultural characteristics, it is through the enculturation or child-rearing process (the cultural transmission process), as well as through interactions in the wider society, that a child's cultural characteristics are established and continuously transformed. Thus, teachers should expect cultural differences both within and between groups (see Gallimore & Goldberg, 2001; Winzer & Mazurek, 1998).

language needs, and identified disabilities. All three are essential: If any one is ignored, the instructional program will suffer. But what does it mean to take into account an English language learner's cultural characteristics and language needs in the context of special education?

This chapter is designed to guide teachers through the complex and necessary instructional planning process. It outlines a process by which special educators can create the following:

- Culturally responsive teaching and learning environments
- Appropriate language and literacy instruction that takes into account the students' stages of development in their first and second languages (including any effects from the disability on language and literacy development) and language use in the home and community
- Sheltered content instruction (an approach using special instructional techniques to make content comprehensible to English language learners) that is planned around the students' second language proficiency and identified disabilities
- A family service plan (FSP) that respects the language and culture of the home and builds on this respect to develop an active partnership between home and school
- An IEP development process that also respects the language and culture of the home

In considering each aspect of the process, this chapter focuses on the practical, day-to-day issues that teachers need to address in their classes. Each aspect that is well integrated into the overall instructional approach adds power to the instruction, which in turn leads to greater teacher and program effectiveness. Therefore, the ability to plan well for students results in student success and parent and teacher satisfaction.

Culturally Responsive Teaching and Learning Environments

Teachers create culturally responsive teaching and learning environments through their efforts in five major areas: curriculum and materials, classroom interactions, teaching approaches, resource management, and counseling and parent outreach efforts.

Curriculum and Materials

By selecting curricular themes and instructional materials that acknowledge the life experiences and background knowledge of the students, instruction can be built on a solid foundation. Students' prior learning experiences, needs, and interests become the basis for creating personally relevant curricula. Multicultural literature is plentiful, and multicultural perspectives reflect the values and beliefs of all children. Materials, both texts and illustrations, are as free of bias or stereotypes as possible, showing respect for all students (García & Malkin, 1993). Culturally biased materials are openly discussed or modified.

An example of culturally responsive curriculum development is available in the work of Luis Moll and colleagues (Moll, Amanti, Neff, & González, 1992), who have demonstrated how the "funds of knowledge" that exist in children's families and communities can be investigated and actively used in classes. Rich interdisciplinary curricula that draw upon the local community's abundant knowledge and skills in particular areas (e.g., agriculture, construction, and service industries) can empower children and families while achieving the school's academic goals.

Culturally relevant materials strongly support the development of literacy. When students read materials with familiar content, their comprehension is enhanced because they can make accurate predictions. Culturally appropriate literature is effective because stories have familiar characters, motives, situations, and settings that conform to students' beliefs, norms, and experiences (Cloud, Genesee, & Hamayan, 2000). Materials that affirm students' identities facilitate student engagement and learning. Familiar themes facilitate personal expression, orally and in writing, because students can draw upon a wealth of ideas. Students are more likely to learn when they are allowed to choose what they read and write about.

An annotated list of resources that will help teachers locate and create culturally and linguistically responsive curricula can be found at the end of this chapter.

Classroom Interactions

The expectations that students have about classroom interactions vary greatly both among and within cultures. Do students expect adult direction and guidance or peer support and feedback? Do they expect interactions to be highly governed by classroom rules or to be more open and flexible? Do they expect their relationship with their teacher to be personal or formal? How do they expect to interact with their peers? In some cultures, public displays of learning are common, whereas in others students feel more confident responding to a peer or privately in writing. Cloud et al. (2000) point out that the following interactional behaviors are known to vary across cultures:

- Amount of adult guidance expected
- Comfort with individual (versus group) response
- Eye contact during instruction
- Comfort with guessing
- Comfort with volunteering in class

Elaborating on the subject, they state,

> Students from some cultural groups have been taught that they should not show off or stand out in the company of others; should not look adults in the eye because it is a sign of disrespect; and should not speak out but rather should learn by watching others. When students behave in these ways, they are doing what is culturally appropriate in their community. Schooling in Anglo-American settings calls for a different set

of behaviors that they will eventually learn. But it will take them time to become comfortable with these new ways of behaving. (Cloud et al., 2000, p. 15)

How can teachers learn about students' expectations? One way is to ask students, through questionnaires or student-teacher conferences, what kinds of conditions they find most favorable for learning. Questions might include the following:

- Do you work better when you receive guidance and direction from the teacher or when you receive support from other students in the class?
- Do you prefer to work alone, with other students, or with the teacher?
- Which would you prefer—answering questions openly in class or telling a partner your response first and then reporting back to the class in teams? (For more information about this technique, see Kinsella, 1996.)

Teachers can also observe the conditions that learners set up for them- selves when they have choices. How many classmates do they choose to work with? Do they choose same-sex or mixed-sex groupings? Do they like to work in cross-age groupings? Do they prefer to be grouped with students from the same ethnic and linguistic background, or do they prefer mixed groupings? Do they seek adult feedback? Is there a lot of talk or little? Do they say more when speaking to an adult or a peer? Do they compare their responses with other students or keep their responses private? Are they motivated by praise from adults, recognition by their classmates, or tangible rewards? What about dis- cipline? Which methods are most culturally compatible?

These are not inconsequential questions to consider because they lead to student comfort in the classroom, motivation to achieve, and active participation, all of which are prerequisites of effective learning (Weisner, Gallimore, & Jordan, 1988). Teachers can also interview cul- tural informants or use other ethnographic means to learn about their students' preferences. They can consult detailed specialized publications (e.g., Lynch & Hanson, 1998; Roseberry-McKibbin, 1995) to learn about traditional values, norms, and behaviors of particular cultural groups, with the understanding that great variation exists within each cultural community.

Once key cultural beliefs, norms, and values have been identified, they can be used to meet important learning goals. One such use is outlined by Turnbull, Pereira, & Blue-Banning (2000). Building on the traditional Hispanic values of *respeto* and *personalismo,* the authors describe strategies that teachers used to promote friendships among students, friendships being a frequent problem for students with disabilities. Effective teachers emphasized the importance of a classroom in which each student is respected and valued. Teachers encouraged early interactions among potential friends and gave continuous support to those interactions, all the while accentuating traditional Hispanic cultural values concerning interpersonal relationships.

Teaching Approaches

Effective teachers choose approaches that are compatible with students' preferences and prior learning experiences (Weisner, Gallimore, & Jordan, 1998). Do students prefer cooperative learning experiences or more traditional teacher-centered approaches? Do students do better with inquiry-based methods that require independence, or do they prefer that the teacher instruct and demonstrate and the students observe and reflect? What about memorization and recitation? Is this a familiar and preferred learning approach, or do learners do better with exploration, investigation, and open discussion? What about student-led instruction? Is this seen as a good way to learn or as an abdication of teacher responsibility? For example, do students welcome process writing instructional approaches in which peers evaluate work and give structured feedback? Or do they feel that the teacher is the only one qualified to perform this instructional role?

Examining the literature, Gersten & Baker (2000) found that effective instruction for English language learners with disabilities used the following techniques:

- New vocabulary to develop a deep understanding of concepts
- Visuals to reinforce new concepts and vocabulary
- Rich and evocative vocabulary to keep students engaged and challenged
- Cooperative learning and peer tutoring methods
- The native language, especially when students are floundering
- Formal and informal opportunities for learners to use English throughout the day
- Feedback that is adapted to the learner's level of language development

In contrast, the following hindered student progress:

- Insufficient time for teaching English
- Insufficient opportunities for students to use oral language and develop English literacy skills
- Insufficient efforts to build students' command of abstract language used in content area instruction
- Insufficient attention to students' cultural differences
- Insufficient attention to students' background knowledge in planning instruction

(For more information on promising instructional practices see Gersten, Baker, & Marks, 1998.)

Asa Hilliard (1992) reminds us that student diversity demands diverse treatment if equitable schooling is to be achieved. For example, which is fairer—to teach all children to read in English (thus allowing some children to learn to read in their native language, while others struggle to read a language they cannot speak) or to teach all children to read in their native languages? If we follow the latter course, we diversify the treatment: One group of children receives reading instruction in

English, while others receive instruction in other languages. Yet the principle undergirding the instruction remains constant: Teach all children to learn to read first in the language in which they are already orally proficient so that they only have to learn the written code. The more that we can honor the accepted principles of child development while meaningfully varying our surface teaching approaches to respond to the unique characteristics of each learner, the more likely we are to succeed. In the current era of educational reform, when the emphasis is on educational outcomes, it is clear that instruction may have to vary widely across groups of children in order to attain the same results. In other words, some children may require special instruction, programs, and services to achieve the same outcomes as other children. (For more information on this topic, see Winzer & Mazurek, 1998.)

Resource Management

Using our resources in culturally responsive ways means using time, space, and people in ways that are sensitive to students. How we organize the daily school schedule makes a difference in how students perform, as does how we arrange the furniture and open spaces in the classroom. Time is used in American classrooms in rather exacting ways (for example, a class period may start at 10:42 and end at 11:19), whereas in other cultures, time is viewed more flexibly, according to the needs of circumstances or participants. Cross-cultural conflicts can arise when teachers expect students to finish their work on time, while students expect the teacher to give them the time they need to complete assignments and to be understanding of all the circumstances that affect their ability to complete work on time. Wait-time is another practice that varies across cultures (Cloud et al., 2000). How long should the teacher wait for a response after asking a question? The standard length of wait-time in the United States may not match other cultural groups' sense of a respectful and adequate amount of time to consider a question and offer a response. This could cause teachers to assume that students cannot respond when, in fact, they have not been given the right conditions to respond.

Likewise, the way the teacher designs classroom space may create comfort or discomfort for the students who inhabit it. Are students' chairs too close together or too far away from each other for students to feel comfortable? Finally, students' access to different instructional staff can be an issue. Does the teacher seem accessible or distant? Do all students have access to the high-status adults in the classroom, or are certain students always assigned to work with individuals, such as paraprofessionals or peer tutors, who are viewed as less important? Teachers can find the answers to these questions by interviewing the students or observing what students do when given choices. Teachers can expect to find variations both between and within groups.

Counseling and Parent Outreach Efforts

Various researchers have documented that not only instruction but also counseling and parent outreach efforts need to be sensitive to students' cultural backgrounds (Cloud, 1993; García, this volume; McGoldrick, Pearce, & Giordano, 1982; Pederson, 1981; Spindler & Spindler, 1994).

For educators working with culturally diverse families, two publications are particularly helpful: *Teaching Language Minority Students in the Multicultural Classroom* by Robin Scarcella (1990) and *Developing Cross-Cultural Competence: A Guide for Working with Young Children and Their Families* by Eleanor W. Lynch and Marci J. Hanson (1998). These references provide valuable information on traditional notions of family life, child rearing, health care practices, and disability across the major cultural groups found in U.S. schools. While understanding that culture is a dynamic and complex phenomenon, professionals will nonetheless find that this information helps them better understand and serve their students.

Appropriate Language and Literacy Instruction

For English language learners with identified disabilities, what is the best way to provide language and literacy development? Should special educators even consider native language instruction as an option, or should English language instruction be offered right from the start?

In planning which language to use for instruction at what points in a student's development, special educators must consider the following:

- The family's language of communication at home
- The learner's stage of development in the first and second languages
- The extent to which the identified disabilities of the learner affect language and literacy development
- The student's current and future needs for both languages
- The strength of each language for instructional purposes (which language better supports learning)
- The language preferences of the learner and the parents

Just because a student has been placed in an English-speaking environment at school does not mean that educators can ignore the native language. On the contrary, a student's native language serves as the foundation for all future language and literacy development, represents an essential part of a student's identity, and links the student to family and community—the other primary learning environment. One of the strongest arguments for strengthening the first language is that by doing so, we create positive conditions for second language learning (Teachers of English to Speakers of Other Languages, 1996).

Researchers have shown that the development of the native language has a positive impact personally, socially, intellectually, educationally, and economically (National Clearinghouse for Bilingual Education, 1996; Teachers of English to Speakers of Other Languages, 1996). Access to and pride in the native language are critical to a child's identity and self-esteem. When the native language is developed and used in school, important links to the family and community are made. High levels of bilingualism are consistently associated with positive cognitive effects, and students who develop their native language as well as English achieve at higher levels than do students whose native language is left to languish, or is replaced, at times prematurely, with English (Collier, 1995a). Even students with identified disabilities seem to benefit from dual language development (Bruck, 1982; Greenlee, 1981). Finally, today's global economy demands individuals who are fluent in languages other than English; those who are bilingual will reap the benefits of better employment opportunities (Carreira & Armengol, 2001).

Special educators can support the development and use of the native language in several ways. They can provide first language instruction to help students develop academically while they are learning English. They can encourage first language development at home. They can welcome the use of the first language at school by having materials available in those languages in the classroom and school library and by featuring them in school publications and communication (Freeman & Freeman, 1993).

What about students with atypical language development or developmental delays? Are these cases any different? Is dual language development out of reach for children with language-based learning disabilities or language disorders? Gutierrez-Clellen (1999) argues that there is no need to avoid use of the home language with students with documented language disorders or language-based disabilities; in fact, the home language should be used as a basis for second language learning. Gutierrez-Clellen favors sequential language learning, in which instruction is first provided in the child's stronger language to facilitate general language learning mechanisms (e.g. attention, perception, and comparison), which in turn support future first and second language learning. According to this design, students are taught in their first language for a predetermined period of time before the second language is introduced. This is contrary to the commonly held belief that if students have difficulties learning language, the native language should be abandoned in favor of the exclusive development of English. Gutierrez-Clellen concludes that "the available literature suggests that intervention approaches may be most successful when they are designed to extend, rather than limit, the child's linguistic resources" (p. 300).

Sequential language and literacy development is recommended for two other important reasons. First, English language learners have been shown to be at risk of remaining at low levels of literacy in both languages or of feeling incompetent if they do not establish a threshold level of competence in their home language first. Second, simultaneous language development often means that too much instructional time is devoted to formal language and literacy instruction in the early grades, which adversely affects achievement in academic subjects (Cloud et al., 2000).

This approach does not deny that functional proficiency in English is an important educational goal for students who live, go to school, and will someday work in the United States. Accordingly, formal second language and literacy instruction should begin as soon as it is developmentally appropriate. Teachers and other language specialists should make that determination after carefully reviewing the student's proficiency in the native language and readiness for formal language instruction in English.

Once English as a second language instruction has begun, instruction can emphasize content-based and cognitive/learning strategies (e.g., Chamot & O'Malley, 1994) for students with mild and moderate disabilities, and lifeskills and vocationally related ESL for students with more severe disabilities. Second language learners with special education needs appear to benefit in particular from multisensory teaching approaches (e.g., Total Physical Response and drama), computer-assisted and other technology-supported instruction, peer tutoring and cooperative learning, learning style-based instruction, and whole language/process approaches (Cloud, 1990, 1994). These methods are recommended because they focus on meaningful communication and have attributes that aid learning and retention. (For additional information about effective second language instruction, see Echevarria & Graves, 1998; Gibbons, 1993; and Peregoy & Boyle, 1997).

Characteristics of Effective Native and Second Language Instruction

The following are characteristics of effective instruction, whether provided in the native language, English, or both languages:

- Instruction is aligned with standards and guided by key learning principles.
- Language is comprehensible, and students have opportunities to interact.
- Language, literacy, and content are integrated.
- Learning objectives are similar in the first and second language.

Aligned With Standards and Guided by Key Learning Principles

Instruction for English language learners with special education needs must meet the same high standards as instruction provided to other children. Thus, to ensure that learners with special education needs are held accountable to the highest possible standards, individualized education program (IEP) goals and objectives should be constructed in relation to state and national curriculum standards, including ESL standards. Teachers working with English language will need to become familiar with the ESL K–12 standards (Teachers of English to Speakers of Other Languages, 1997) in order to design appropriate language and literacy goals. Once students achieve proficiency in English, the state's adopted language arts standards can be applied. If some of the state-adopted standards are immediately appropriate, both sets of standards can be included in the IEP goals and objectives.

Gersten & Baker (2000) recommend a balanced English language development program that includes the development of both social language (natural conversational language) and academic language, along with traditional language study (vocabulary and syntax), all while assisting learners to use language in socially and culturally appropriate ways. These goals are consistent with the three broad goals that Teachers of English to Speakers of Other Languages (1997) has set for English language learners: to develop social language, academic language, and sociocultural competence. These goals should be reflected in students' IEPs. In addition, we know that language learning is a long-term process that occurs through meaningful use and that language use processes (listening, speaking, reading, and writing) develop interdependently (Teachers of English to Speakers of Other Languages, 1996). These general principles of language acquisition provide direction to our work in classrooms and help us to set appropriate expectations and design appropriate learning experiences for second language learners, including those with special education needs. (For more guidance on this topic, including model instructional units, see Irujo, 2000; Wertheimer & Honigsfeld, 2000.)

Comprehensible Language in Interactive Classrooms

Effective teachers modify their language so that it is comprehensible to students. They use natural redundancy, carefully constructed language to match student proficiency, and "layered or augmented communication" (use of physical gestures, visual cues, props, and realia) to ensure communication (Gersten & Woodward, 1994). At the same time, they provide opportunities for students to use the new language. This might involve the use of cooperative learning groups to maximize language use and to allow new language forms and modes of expression to be internalized. In face-to-face interactions, learners can get feedback about their performance in nonthreatening conditions. Active learning and peer support have been shown to greatly enhance language learning for English language learners (Fern, Anstrom, & Silcox, 1994).

Integrated Language, Literacy, and Content Instruction

Because context-rich learning is preferred, lessons should be designed to integrate content and language learning. Such lessons contain four objectives: linguistic, communicative, content, and learning strategies and study skills. Once the learning objectives are established, activities and materials are selected with cultural appropriateness and the students' disabilities in mind. (See discussion on sheltered content instruction below.) For example, in a unit about weather, the four learning objectives might be those listed in Figure 1.

Gersten & Baker (2000) recommend that educators improve the ways they integrate content area instruction and language instruction since their research revealed that current attempts to integrate the two are not well implemented. They urge teachers to provide sufficient time for teaching English and for students to use oral and written language to acquire academic content. (For more guidance on this topic, see Echevarria, Vogt, & Short, 2000).

FIGURE **1**

> *Linguistic:* to learn the terms sunny, windy, cloudy, rainy, foggy, hot, dry, humid, clear, warm, cold, nice; the phrases "What's it like outside?", "How's the weather today?", "It's ___. ", "I like/hate it when it's ___"; and grammar focus: adverbs/adjectives, present tense of the verb to be, wh- questions, when clauses, contractions.
>
> *Communicative* (linked with the Teachers of English to Speakers of Other Languages ESL Standards): to describe weather conditions in terms of temperature, amount and type of precipitation, humidity, wind velocity, and visibility, orally and in writing (Goal 2, Standard 2); to request or supply information about the weather (Goal 1, Standard 1); and to express likes and dislikes about the weather (Goal 2, Standard 1).
>
> *Content:* to learn the scientific causes of weather conditions (cloud cover, types of precipitation, air pressure, wind velocity, temperature, humidity, weather fronts, and severe weather conditions); to learn about weather forecasting and weather forecasts.
>
> *Learning Strategies/Study Skills:* to use the newspaper, radio, TV, and the Internet to locate information about the weather in various parts of the world; to produce tables, charts, and graphs to illustrate local weather conditions; and to work effectively with others to record and report on weather conditions.

Objectives for Integrated Language, Literacy, and Content Instruction in a Unit on the Weather

Similar Learning Objectives in the First and Second Language

When the language of the home and the school differ, teachers and parents can work together by focusing on those objectives that are not specific to one language. Using the example of weather, this would mean that teachers and parents would both work on the same communicative objective (e.g., to request or supply information about the weather), content objective (e.g., to learn about weather forecasting), and learning strategy/study skill objective (e.g., to use the newspaper or the Internet to locate information), leaving only the linguistic objectives to vary according to the language used in each learning environment. Such efforts strengthen the instructional program because the home and school are working together toward the same end.

Sheltered Content Instruction

Sheltered content instruction involves making academic content comprehensible to English language learners. It is a multiphase process when working with learners with special education needs. This is because teachers must think through how they will shelter the instruction for students' second language needs and then how they will modify the instruction for the identified disabilities. Through this two-step sheltering process, teachers can accommodate all of the student's primary needs.

In order to make content area instruction comprehensible to English language learners, Zehler (1994) advises teachers to do the following:

- Create an accepting and predictable environment by using structured activities and letting students know what is expected of them.
- Maximize opportunities for language use by asking carefully constructed questions that students can answer.
- Create opportunities for student dialogue in a supportive environment.
- Encourage active participation. Give students responsibility for their own learning, use discovery processes and cooperative learning,

make learning relevant to the students' experience, use thematic teaching, and design activities that promote use of learning strategies and higher order thinking skills.

- Support understanding by guiding and facilitating learning efforts, adapting speech to students' proficiency levels, using multimodal instruction (e.g., visuals, realia, and graphic organizers) to ensure understanding, offering peer support, and using the native language (e.g., through the use of instructional aides and students who speak the language) to clarify meaning or to expand learning.

In addition, teachers can use the following:

- Vocabulary guides, semantic webs, concept maps, advance organizers, and structured overviews to help students develop the vocabulary and background knowledge needed to understand academic content
- Guided reading strategies with English textbooks or select materials that are linguistically appropriate for students' stages of language proficiency
- Strategies (such as guided questioning, prediction, and graphic aids) that support reading comprehension
- Structured study guides, information organizers, chapter outlines, and short summary notes to record key concepts
- Reciprocal (peer-mediated or adult-directed) teaching techniques to help students acquire key concepts and the related academic language (Kang, 1994; Leverett & Diefendorf, 1992)

To shelter instruction for English language learners with special education needs, teachers can do the following:

- Create a learner-friendly environment through seating and lighting.
- Remove distractions to student learning.
- Vary classroom organization and management tactics to provide needed support and encouragement.

- Adapt methods of presentation (e.g., use modeling and demonstration) and methods of practice (visual, auditory, kinesthetic, and tactile presentation of new concepts) to the students' needs.
- Use technology to enhance learning.
- Apply behavior management techniques.
- Use reformatted materials (graphic organizers, enlarged typeface, cued text, and recorded books) and technology aids.
- Use one-on-one teaching through the use of cross-age and peer tutoring and instructional aides.

In terms of assessment in sheltered content classes, a particularly fruitful approach is portfolio assessment, which uses a variety of products and information-gathering techniques, such as anecdotal records, language samples, and interviews with students and parents, to create a picture of student progress over time. Portfolio assessment has been strongly advocated by specialists familiar with the needs of culturally and linguistically diverse special education students (Salend, 1998; Swicegood, 1994). A clear advantage of portfolio assessment, according to its advocates, is its compatibility with the IEP. (For a comprehensive treatment of sheltering instruction for English language learners with and without special education needs, see Echevarria et al., 2000; Echevarria & Graves, 1998; Santamaria et al., this volume.)

A Culturally and Linguistically Responsive Family Service Plan

Greene and Nefsky (1999) suggest that educators consider the following when establishing partnerships with families from culturally and linguistically diverse backgrounds:

- The family's level of acculturation
- The family's attitudes toward disability and their acceptance of their child with a disability
- The family's communication style and the possible need for communication to take place in a language other than English

- The family's knowledge of and comfort with the school infrastructure (e.g., special education procedures, school personnel roles and responsibilities, and parental rights)
- The family's perceptions of school (based on their prior experience and cultural expectations) as well as the value they place on education
- Special education professionals' knowledge of and sensitivity to cultural diversity

(Greene & Nefsky, 1999, p. 16)

In thinking through the family service plan (FSP), a fundamental consideration in working with culturally diverse families is how the term *family* is defined and who should be involved in the decision-making process, as many different family configurations are possible in a culturally diverse society. School personnel need to consider other cultural factors as well. These include the preferred communication style (e.g., direct versus indirect communication), the level of trust that must be established before "business" can be conducted, and the preference for face-to-face communication or written communication (Greene & Nefsky, 1999; Harry, 1992). When preparing written documents, including routine correspondence or procedural guides (regarding, for example, special education services and due process rights), specialists recommend that educators consider a family's specific language and cultural situation. Assessing a family's literacy level and modifying materials to make them more comprehensible is essential. (For a discussion of how format and message considerations can improve document comprehension among culturally diverse families, see Boone, Wolfe, & Schaufler, 1999).

Meaningful IEPs for English Language Learners

The Individualized Education Plan (IEP) is the annual planning tool that establishes the long-term goals for a given academic year, whereas lesson and unit plans are the day-to-day planning tools that teachers use to attain the IEP goals. All planning tools should show evidence of teachers' thoughtful consideration of the backgrounds and needs of their students and of meaningful outreach to their families.

The 1997 Individuals With Disabilities Act Amendments required some major changes in the ways that IEPs are developed for all learners. The amendments expand the roles of parents and regular classroom teachers. They also describe the extent of student participation in the general curriculum and in statewide and district assessments. Schools must regularly inform parents of their children's progress and closely monitor students' annual goals throughout the year.

According to Cooper and Rascon (1994), *informed consent* means that it is the responsibility of the school to ensure that all parents—regardless of their educational, cultural, and language backgrounds—understand the school's instructional services. Educators must make sure that parents not only consent to the instructional services outlined in the IEP, but that they are able to contribute to the effectiveness of their child's program and understand and endorse its goals. Given the enhanced role of parents, some tips for effective IEP meetings are listed in Figure 2.

Likewise, all school staff participating in the development of the IEP must be knowledgeable about appropriate educational services for students from culturally and linguistically diverse backgrounds, and all assessments must be conducted in culturally and linguistically valid and reliable ways.

The IEP can specify if special education and related services will be provided in English or the native language. Technology, instructional aides, and instructional services should be provided to the same extent that they are provided to English-speaking students with similar needs. To make assessment more equitable for second language learners, tests can be modified. Adapting the language of the test, screening items for content bias, and providing sufficient time to process and produce the second language are three such modifications.

FIGURE **2** ■

- Conduct the meeting in a comfortable location. Invite parents or guardians to bring a trusted friend/advisor to the meeting.

- Conduct the meeting in the parents' language with translation into English for school personnel. Allow sufficient time, so that the parents do not feel rushed. Don't overwhelm parents with too many school personnel at the meeting.

- Determine if the parents have any concerns for the education of their child prior to establishing the annual goals and objectives.

- Offer educational options to parents regarding their child's education, and solicit their input about the various options. Invite parents to visit school at any time to see how their child is doing in the various programs and services.

- Make sure that parents understand and accept the plan.

- Offer guidance and support to families as to how they can contribute to the attainment of IEP goals.

- Prepare all documents in a way that communicates effectively with parents. Use their most proficient language and make certain that they are provided a copy as soon as possible after the meeting (see Boone, Wolfe, & Schaufler, 1999).

Tips for IEP Meetings

Conclusion

Language, culture, and disability define English language learners with special education needs, and all three must be accommodated through the instructional planning process. When teachers plan instruction, they need to take each into account individually, while keeping the goal of integrated instruction in mind. Not only do they need to fit instruction as much as possible to the cultural, linguistic, and personal profiles of students, but they also need to reach out to their families in a culturally and linguistically responsive manner so that home and school become mutually reinforcing learning environments. Through systematic instructional planning, all of these important goals can be accomplished.

Resources for Developing a Culturally and Linguistically Responsive Curriculum

Brown, D. S. (1994). *Books for a small planet.* Alexandria, VA: Teachers of English to Speakers of Other Languages.

> A multicultural bibliography for pre-K–12 students that includes descriptions of trade books (fiction and nonfiction) with diverse settings and characters. Designed to help teachers select books to complement the topics they are teaching or to fit into particular genres of literature being taught.

De Cou-Landberg, M. (1994). *The global classroom: A thematic multicultural model for the K–6 and ESL classroom* (Volumes 1 & 2). Reading, MA: Addison-Wesley.

> A resource book of model interdisciplinary thematic units with multilevel activities and resources. Using a multisensory teaching/learning approach, ideas are provided for developing language and literacy across the content areas and for working effectively with families. Stresses active learning, process, and project-based approaches. Developed by an experienced and creative ESL teacher.

DeGaetano, Y., Williams, L. R., & Volk, D. (1988). *Kaleidoscope: A multicultural approach for the primary school classroom.* Upper Saddle River, NJ: Merrill, Prentice-Hall.

> A practical and comprehensive approach to working with K–3 children of diverse backgrounds to develop language and support academic learning. Anchored in the lives and communities of children, the authors offer rich examples of how to develop culturally, linguistically, and personally relevant curriculum and instruction. Excellent chapters on setting up the classroom, involving parents, assessing student progress, and advocating for multicultural teaching in schools. A variety of useful tools are provided in the appendices.

Hollins, E. R. (1996). *Culture in school learning: Revealing the deep meaning.* Mahwah, NJ: Lawrence Erlbaum.

> Discusses the centrality of culture in school learning; ways of acquiring meaningful data from teachers, students, and parents for curricular and instructional planning; and suggestions for reframing, redesigning, and transforming curriculum and instruction to create supportive and meaningful learning in K–12.

Igoa, C. (1995). *The inner world of the immigrant child.* Mahwah, NJ: Lawrence Erlbaum.

> Using the stories of fifth- and sixth-grade children, the teacher describes her sheltered English approach, which responds to students' affective, linguistic, and academic needs. A very moving look at children's transition to English and the kinds of classroom practices that aid them in that journey.

Kezwer, P. (1995). *Worlds of wonder: Resources for multicultural children's literature.* Scarborough, Ontario: Pippin Press.

> Developed by a Canadian ESL teacher, this detailed listing of more than 300 titles aids teachers in presenting the experience of major immigrant groups, as well as in locating books from particular geographic regions of the world. Cross-referenced listings by author, title, and theme are provided. Each book is categorized by age appropriateness.

Kucer, S. B., Silva, C., & Delgado-Larocco, E. L. (1995). *Curricular conversations: Themes in multilingual and monolingual classrooms.* York, ME: Stenhouse.

> Provides a model of curriculum integration for bilingual and sheltered English classrooms that is anchored in the conceptual development of learners. Describes how teachers can develop a conceptually sound and integrated thematic curriculum in their classrooms. A variety of model units are described; each includes a listing of resources in Spanish and English.

Lynch, E. W., & Hanson, M. J. (1998). *Developing cross-cultural competence: A guide for working with young children and their families* (2nd
ed.). Baltimore: Paul H. Brookes.
    This book provides important background information about
    the contemporary lifestyles, values, and beliefs of major ethnic
    and cultural groups. It provides descriptions of child-rearing
    and health care practices and beliefs about disability.

Moll, L., Amanti, C. A., Neff, D., & González, N. (1992). Funds of
knowledge for teaching: Using a qualitative approach to connect
homes and classrooms. *Theory into Practice, 31*(2), 132-141.
    An ethnographic approach to building curriculum and instruc-
    tion that validates the rich life experience and knowledge base
    of children, families, and communities.

Santos, R. M., Fowler, S. A., Corso, R. B., & Bruns, D. A. (2000).
Acceptance, acknowledgment, and adaptability: Selecting culturally
and linguistically appropriate early childhood materials. *Teaching
Exceptional Children, 32*(3), 14-22.
    Offers practical guidelines for selecting and adapting materi-
    als for use with culturally and linguistically diverse families
    with special needs children. Tips for effective translation are
    included. Copyright issues are also addressed.

Scarcella, R. (1990). *Teaching language minority students in the multicultural classroom.* Englewood Cliffs, NJ: Prentice Hall Regents.
    Though published in 1990, this is a basic book for teachers
    that covers key topics such as understanding second language
    acquisition, developing comprehensible lessons, and testing
    and teaching in culturally responsive ways.

Taylor, S. V. (2000). Multicultural is who we are: Literature as a reflection of ourselves. *Teaching Exceptional Children, 32*(3), 14-22.
    Offers tips and tools to teachers to assist them in selecting
    multicultural literature from a global perspective. Particular
    representative books are reviewed, and useful bibliographies
    are provided.

Multicultural Book Review Home Page
<http://www.isomedia.com/homes/jmele/homepage.html>
> An access page to multicultural links and book reviews (categorically listed).

Center for Multilingual Multicultural Research
<http://www-bcf.usc.edu/~cmmr/BEResources.html>
> A rich collection of bilingual, ESL and multicultural education resources and links.

Effective Pedagogy for English Language Learners in Inclusive Classrooms

Lorri Johnson Santamaría, *California State University San Marcos*
Todd V. Fletcher, *University of Arizona*
Candace S. Bos, *University of Texas at Austin*

According to the National Institute of Human Development (1998), 15% of the U.S. population, or 1 in 7 Americans, have some type of learning disability. A learning disability (LD) has been defined as a neurobiological disorder that interferes with the ability to learn and remember. A learning disability can affect a person's ability to speak, listen, read, write, spell, reason, recall, organize information, and perform mathematical operations. Although the federal definition stipulates that students not be identified as learning disabled when their learning patterns can be attributed primarily to cultural and linguistic diversity, students are often evaluated using approaches that are culturally and linguistically inappropriate (Gutiérrez & Stone, 1997). Factors such as English language proficiency, level of acculturation, and method of classroom instruction can be overlooked in the special education referral, assessment, and qualifying process for English language learners. To ignore these factors is to contribute to the overrepresentation of learners from culturally and linguistically diverse backgrounds in special education programs (Artiles, Trent, Hoffman-Kipp, & López-Torres, 2000).

A definition of a learning disability from a sociocultural perspective takes cultural and linguistic variables into consideration. "The basic goal of the sociocultural (cultural and historical) approach is to create an account of human mental processes that recognizes the essential relationship between these processes and their cultural, historical, and institutional settings" (Wertsch, 1991, p. 6). According to this theory, societal factors (e.g., race and socioeconomic class) and structural factors within the education system (e.g., shifting standards and inappropriate teaching methodologies), may cause academicunder achievement that is incorrectly interpreted by educators to indicate learning disabilities (Coles, 1987; Sleeter, 1986). These factors are particularly critical when considering students who are English language learners.

For English language learners who qualify for special education support, the way that instruction is delivered can either enhance learning or exacerbate learning difficulties (Ruiz, García, & Figueroa, 1996). When included in general education classes, English language learners with learning difficulties are often considered less proficient academically than other learners—that is, English-speaking peers with or without disabilities, native speakers of other languages, and bilingual peers without disabilities. If English language learners with learning disabilities are to benefit from instruction, a critical question becomes, What kind of instruction should be provided?

This chapter describes an alternative approach to language arts instruction that includes scaffolding strategies, effective pedagogy, and dual language instruction for English language learners with learning disabilities who are included in general education classes. The chapter begins with a description of scaffolding for English language learners with learning disabilities, followed by a description of four scaffolding strategies and five principles for effective pedagogy. It concludes with classroom-based applications of the strategies and principles by two third-grade teachers whose goals were to meet the needs of English language learners with learning disabilities in their general education classes.

Scaffolding for English Language Learners With Learning Disabilities

Scaffolding is what a teacher, adult assistant, or more capable peer does when working with a student "to solve a problem, carry out a task, or achieve a goal which would be beyond their unassisted efforts" (Wood, Bruner, & Ross, 1976, p. 90). In general education classes that include English language learners with learning disabilities, more proficient individuals—teachers, adult assistants, or student peers—can provide scaffolds for these learners. Similar to a builder's scaffold, scaffolding provides a temporary structure that helps learners make cognitive connections. Unlike the rigid scaffolds used in the construction of a building, educational scaffolds are fluid, dynamic, and interactive. They can be used to temporarily assist both English language learners with learning disabilities and academically proficient students, as they develop knowledge, understanding, strategies, and skills. These interactive scaffolds can gradually be removed as students start to learn more independently.

How Scaffolding Strategies Work

Educational tools that support student learning are scaffolds. These tools, such as story maps, paragraph frames, and sentence starters, include templates that aid students in their learning. Scaffolds shift from outwardly visible or external to abstract or internal. In other words, supports that are originally provided externally by teachers or more proficient peers are replaced by internalized strategies that are used independently by the students.

Other types of scaffolding naturally occur in the classroom as well as at home. For example, in the classroom a teacher organizes information, such as names, dates, assignments, and activity times, to provide students with an overview of the day as well as to help them organize their school day. By high school, college, or adult life, most people have internalized these organizational behaviors and keep calendars, Palm Pilots, day planners, or other methods of time management.

The teaching of telephone etiquette at home is another example of scaffolding for children. Children are first exposed to the unspoken rules of telephone use by listening to adults and older siblings answer the phone. Later, before they answer a telephone on their own, children usually have the opportunity to talk with a relative who naturally models a telephone conversation for them. When children finally have the opportunity to answer the phone by themselves, the caller often facilitates their participation by helping them through a conversation that results in the caller reaching the desired member of the household. Eventually, most children internalize telephone etiquette and are able to use telephones without the mediated scaffolds.

The Zone of Proximal Development

Scaffolding strategies can be used most effectively in what Vygotsky (1978) called the zone of proximal development (ZPD), in which less proficient learners rely on the assistance of more capable individuals to achieve tasks that they would not be able to achieve without such support. Teachers help students move through the ZPD by involving them in activities that require them to perform skills and use strategies before they have mastered them. To teach in the ZPD is to be responsive to learners' goals and stages of development and to provide guidance and assistance that enables learners to achieve their goals while increasing their potential for independent academic work (Wells, 1998).

Scaffolding within a learner's ZPD is especially important for English language learners, with or without learning disabilities, because it builds upon their language, culture, and prior experiences. The student's first language, for example, can serve as a scaffold for learning a second language. By supporting the connections between funds of knowledge at home and what is taught at school, scaffolding promotes learning (González et al, 1993; Moll, Amanti, Neff, & González, 1992).

Four Scaffolding Strategies

Research suggests that English language learners use specific strategies to help them transfer information from Spanish to English (Chamot & O'Malley, 1996). Researchers working in English language learning and in special education have found that scaffolding is an effective strategy for transferring knowledge from the first to the second language (Echevarria & Graves, 1998; Gersten & Jiménez, 1998). Thus, scaffolding appears to work effectively as a strategy for English language learners with learning disabilities.

Englert and Marriage (1996) describe three types of scaffolding strategies: mediated scaffolds, task scaffolds, and materials scaffolds. A fourth, more abstract scaffolding strategy is the use of comprehensible input to promote second language acquisition (Krashen, 1982a, 1982b).

Mediated Scaffolds

With mediated scaffolds, the teacher, the teacher's aide, or a more proficient peer helps to make new information and tasks accessible to the student. Assistance is gradually withdrawn, and responsibility is systematically transferred to the student. For example, a teacher-directed series of mini-lessons on adjectives could help a student understand the process of adjective use. The mini-lessons might feature a class brainstorming session on nouns and adjectives, followed by a session of students working with peers to generate lists of adjectives. The lesson might culminate with students independently generating and using adjectives in writing and other assignments.

Task Scaffolds

These scaffolds shape the ways a task is carried out. They allow students with learning disabilities to focus on their learning process and strategies by reducing the information that they must generate independently. In language arts, for example, students might be given pictures on cue cards that depict the steps they need to follow to complete an activity. Eventually, the students will be able to independently compose summaries, stories, or descriptions without the cue cards.

Materials Scaffolds

Materials scaffolds are strategically designed advanced organizers (e.g., story maps, paragraph frames, and sentence starters) that gradually provide less and less support, resulting in the student's ability to create a product with little or no support. Initially, materials scaffolds may be completed by the teacher on chart paper or transparencies with input from students. Eventually, students are given opportunities to work with these scaffolds independently.

A story map, used to teach the skill of organizing the different elements of a story into a cohesive whole, is an example of an advanced organizer (see Figure 1). The story map is a chart with spaces for the story's title, characters, setting, beginning, middle, and end. Initially, the teacher might complete the map with student help. Then students might fill in the spaces with the appropriate information with the teacher's help. Eventually, students are able to put the components of the map together themselves and write a complete story. Once they are proficient with the story map components, they can use blank charts to organize story components themselves. After they have internalized the writing process, students are able to formulate ideas for a story using blank paper and drawing their own version of an advanced organizer. In this way, students progress from limited proficiency to proficiency with a materials scaffold to proficiency without a scaffold.

Comprehensible Input

A concept that seems compatible with scaffolding strategies is comprehensible input (Krashen, 1982a, 1982b). Developed to explain one aspect of second language acquisition, comprehensible input is language used in ways that make it understandable and meaningful to the language learner. Comprehensible input can be viewed as a scaffolding strategy that enables students to more readily acquire a second

FIGURE **1**

Title:
Characters:
Setting:
Beginning (conflict):
Middle:
End (resolution):

Story Map

language within a well-supported zone of proximal development. For example, in presenting the concept of simple fractions, a teacher might pair key vocabulary (e.g., *whole, half,* and *quarter*) with concrete demonstrations using manipulatives.

Figure 2 lists all four scaffolds with descriptions and examples of each. The examples provided are developed more completely throughout the chapter.

Five Guiding Principles for Effective Pedagogy

Research tells educators what tasks to do when teaching English language learners with learning disabilities in general education classrooms, but it seldom tells teachers how to carry out the tasks (Gersten & Jiménez, 1998). A group of researchers in California (Tharp, Estrada, Dalton, & Yamauchi, 2000) has developed five principles that can be helpful for both special educators and general educators who have English language learners in their classes.

FIGURE **2** ■

Scaffold Type	Description	Examples
Mediated Activities	Support provided by teacher or more proficient peer, who intervenes and helps less proficient learner learn new information	Teacher-directed mini-lessons, buddy reading, cooperative learning groups
Tasks	Support embedded in the tasks, allowing students to focus on learning process and strategies, reducing information they must generate independently	Student-friendly instructions for task completion
Materials	Support provided through strategically designed prompts for learners	Story maps, paragraph frames, sentence starters
Comprehensible Input	Language used in ways that make it understandable to the learner while developing second language proficiency	Information presented and available in students' first or second language to increase understanding

Four Scaffolding Strategies for English Language Learners With Learning Disabilities

The five principles are as follow:

- Work collaboratively with students.
- Develop language and literacy across the curriculum.
- Connect school to students' lives.
- Teach complex thinking.
- Teach through conversation.

Tharp and his researchers found that in classes where these principles are applied, students achieve at much higher levels. Jiménez and Gersten (1999) found similar principles to be important for successfully teaching English language learners with learning disabilities in general education classes. Combined, these two sets of principles provide a framework within which to view scaffolding for these learners. Figure 3 shows how these principles and scaffolds intersect.

FIGURE **3** ▪

Guiding Principles	Scaffolding Strategies
Work collaboratively with students/ Create a community of learners	*Mediated:* buddy reading, cooperative learning groups, teachers and other adults facilitating center work
Develop language and literacy across the curriculum/ Use multiple techniques to promote second language acquisition	*Materials:* advanced organizers *Comprehensible input:* language that is understandable to students in their second language
Connect school to students' lives/ Incorporate cultural diversity into instruction	*Task:* information embedded in task that helps students perform task *Comprehensible input:* language that is understandable to students in their first or second language
Teach complex thinking/ Engage in cognitively challenging activities	*Mediated:* cognitively challenging teacher-directed mini-lessons
Teach through conversation/ Foster extended discourse	*Mediated:* teacher-directed mini-lessons, cooperative learning activities

Guiding Principles for Effective Pedagogy and Scaffolding Strategies
See Tharp, Estrada, Dalton, & Yamauchi, 2000; Jiménez & Gersten, 1999.

Scaffolding Strategies and Principles of Pedagogy at Work

The use of scaffolding strategies and principles of effective pedagogy can best be shown in the context of actual classes—in this case, two third-grade, dual language instruction (Spanish and English) language arts classes in an elementary school in the U.S. Southwest.

The Teachers and Students

The classes were taught by Lena and Marta (pseudonyms), second-year bilingual teachers. Their goal was to explore the use of scaffolding strategies for one academic semester to meet the needs of all of their students, including English language learners with learning disabilities. Both teachers considered their classes to be challenging teaching environments. More than 90% of the 650 students attending the school were on free or reduced lunch programs, with 93% of the population being Hispanic, 2% American Indian, and 5% representing other language groups, including English speakers. The community where the school is located is transitional, as many immigrant families remain there only long enough to become financially stable, at which time they move elsewhere in the city.

Both Lena and Marta had a wide variety of students in their classes. There were monolingual Spanish speakers, monolingual English speakers, and students at various stages of learning English and Spanish. Gifted and talented students studied in the same class with students with disabilities. English language learners with learning disabilities attended resource programs for 1 hour daily. For the rest of the time, they were fully included in the general education classes, with accommodations made for them depending on their needs and the sensitivity and skills of the teachers.

The school district philosophy encouraged site-based management. With regard to English language learners, the site management team had decided that teachers were responsible for literacy instruction in the students' first language in Grades 1 through 3. For language arts instruction, students were regrouped based on their proficiency in their first language, with Marta teaching language arts in Spanish and Lena teaching it in English. In accordance with the district's late exit transitional model of bilingual education (Collier, 1995b), the site management team designated the fourth grade as the grade that Spanish-speaking students would make the transition into English language instruction.

The Problem

Lena and Marta were not satisfied with the school plan, which segregated language arts instruction by language background so that until fourth grade, Spanish speakers with or without learning disabilities received their instruction in Spanish, while English speakers with or without learning disabilities received their instruction in English. Lena and Marta were interested in applying in their diverse classes some of the research and practices they had learned during teacher preparation. Both were concerned about the abrupt transition to English instruction in the fourth grade for the Spanish speakers and about the standardized assessments given in English in the fourth grade. They were especially concerned about their students with learning disabilities.

The Solution

The school plan was based on the assumption that the development of conversational skills must precede the development of academic language proficiency, thus delaying the transition of second language learners into academic work. Lena and Marta questioned this assumption. They believed that through the use of scaffolding strategies and the five guiding principles for effective pedagogy, and with proper first language support and consistent instruction in both languages, English language learners, including those with disabilities, could perform at challenging levels earlier than the 7 to 10 years purportedly required to develop CALP (Collier, 1995b; Cummins, 1994a). Lena and Marta decided to use scaffolding strategies during their own language arts instruction as a way to introduce cognitively challenging concepts with basic communication skills and to teach English more effectively to all of their students.

Lena and Marta's Plan

Lena and Marta decided to do four things. First, they selected several scaffolding strategies and incorporated them into their language arts classes. Second, they taught the strategies to the students for several weeks until they could use them in their first language. Third, they combined equal numbers of Spanish and English speakers in a language arts class and encouraged them to explore ways to apply the strategies they had developed in their first language to their second language (English for Spanish speakers and Spanish for English speakers). Fourth, they carefully monitored the students' progress (especially that of the English language learners with learning disabilities) with student portfolios, checklists, and anecdotal records.

First Language Instruction

Lena and Marta's instruction took place in two phases: first language instruction (Spanish for Spanish speakers and English for English speakers) and then dual language (English and Spanish) instruction. The purpose of first language instruction, which lasted from August to January, was to provide students with sufficient scaffolding strategies for them to learn new language arts content and acquire scaffolding strategies that would be useful for second language learning. The first language instruction phase was especially important for English language learners with learning disabilities because they had many opportunities to use different types of scaffolding strategies. Figure 4 shows a unit plan for the first language instruction phase.

Dual Language Instruction

During dual language instruction, which lasted from January to June, Spanish and English speakers worked together to help each other develop their language proficiency. During this phase of instruction, all learners, including those with learning disabilities, were both second language learners and language experts; which one a student was at any particular time depended on the activity. Students participated in activities similar to those they had done during the first language instruction phase, but now they were using their first languages at times and their second languages at other times. Figure 5 gives a week-long plan for dual language instruction, showing the activities in which the students were engaged.

Scaffolding Strategies in Action

Lena and Marta incorporated all four types of scaffolds into their teaching.

Mediated Scaffolds

The mediated scaffolds that Lena and Marta used in both first language and dual language instruction were buddy reading, cooperative groups, and center work (see Figure 5). For buddy reading in both first and dual language instruction, less proficient readers were paired with more proficient readers, who acted as peer experts, providing assistance when necessary. During dual language instruction, reading buddies with different first languages were paired so that both English and Spanish language learners could have a native speaker help them with their second language learning.

Rob (a pseudonym), the LD resource teacher, was one of the adults who facilitated learning in Lena's classes during first language instruction. In the writing center, he guided students during a 2-week project in the use of paragraph frames (see Figure 6) to plan and write a descriptive paragraph about the story *Bringing the Rain to Kapiti Plain*. Throughout the project, Rob scaffolded the instruction. Depending on student needs, he elicited rich descriptive language from the students, guided them in developing initial drafts by modeling and assisting, and modeled an editing strategy called COPS: capitalization, overall organization, punctuation, and spelling (Schumaker, Nolan, & Deshler, 1985).

FIGURE **4** ■

Language Arts	Goals and Procedures	Accommodations	Materials	Evaluation
Spelling Teacher/Facilitator: Ms. Murray Spelling Words — patches — hatch — scratch — plain — grain — pain — ground — sounds — pounding — wounded — wound — eagle — lean — terrible — horrible	*Objective:* Students produce rainbow words (an activity that uses crayons to teach sound and symbol correspondences) with spelling words to prepare for spelling test. • Adult gives guidelines for center and elicits word pattern and meaning dialogue. • Students practice spelling words by writing each word three times with different colored crayons and then on the back of the paper from memory. • Adult assesses the small group.	*LD Students:* Students may not complete all words and will not be penalized. *Gifted/Accelerated Students:* Students may have time to test each other before the "official" test.	Pencils, paper, and crayons	• Spelling test administered by adult • Spelling grade given (number of words attempted vs. number of words correct)

First Language Instruction, Language Arts, Third Grade, Unit Plan

FIGURE **4**
continued

Language Arts	Goals and Procedures	Accommodations	Materials	Evaluation
Reading Teacher/Facilitator: Ms. Lena	*Objective:* Students complete group reading comprehension activity for *Bringing the Rain to Kapiti Plain.* • Adult introduces activity, explaining that each person in the center will use a different color pen so that it is clear who participated. • Adult reads through, explaining each question. • Students complete activity.	*LD and Gifted/ Accelerated Students:* Adult is integral to this center for modeling and reading directions, modifying the activity to match the individual needs of the students, and participating using instructional conversations. The activity is simplified and reduced for LD students and made more challenging for gifted/accelerated students.	Copies of the activity	Adult completes checklist of desired behaviors: • Cooperates • Stays on task • Participates • Completes task • Grading rubric for activities based on 4-point scale. 4 pts = A 3 pts = B 2 pts = C 1 pt = D

First Language Instruction, Language Arts, Third Grade, Unit Plan (continued)

FIGURE **4**
continued

Language Arts	Goals and Procedures	Accommodations	Materials	Evaluation
Writing Teacher/Facilitator: Mr. Rob	*Objective:* Students write descriptive paragraphs about the story on the computer, using a paragraph frame. • Adult sets up computers. • Students type work from paragraph frames from previous week. • Students proofread work using COPS. • Students print work.	*LD Students:* Scaffold is provided by paragraph frame and adult facilitator. *Gifted/Accelerated Students:* Students may opt to write paragraphs without scaffold or write descriptive expository texts including several paragraphs.	Paragraph frames completed the previous week Additional support materials if necessary	Adult completes checklist of desired behaviors: • Cooperates • Stays on task • Participates • Completes task
Listening, Art, and Creative Expression Teacher/Facilitator: Ms. Berta	*Objective:* Students create texts for animal picture pop-up books they created in the center. • Adult models and explains. • Students create stories and share work.	*LD Students:* Adult is available for scaffolding if necessary. *Gifted/Accelerated Students:* Students may also write poems or plays to accompany their projects.	Construction paper Glue Scissors Paper	Presentation to small group checklist: • Loud voice • Eye Contact • Full page coverage • Quality work

First Language Instruction, Language Arts, Third Grade, Unit Plan (continued)

GURE **5** ■

English Language Learners	Major Dual Language Activities 9:30–10:15 Daily	Spanish Language Learners
8:30–8:45 *Free Reading of English texts* Students read silently books that they have chosen.	**Monday** *Wordless Texts* • Six groups of students write the words for stories in their second language. • Stories are edited by language "experts." • If time permits, students present their stories to the class.	8:30–8:45 *Free Reading of Spanish texts* Students read silently books that they have chosen.
8:45–9:00 *Personal Dictionary* Students add at least 8 words from their free reading story to their personal dictionary.	**Tuesday** *ABC Books* Students create ABC books in their second language with magazine cut outs and simple sentences (2 letters per student).	8:45–9:00 *Personal Dictionary* Students add at least 8 words from their free reading story to their personal dictionary.
9:00–9:15 *Buddy Reading* Students read their English language book to one English-speaking student.	**Wednesday** *Literature Circles* • Six groups of students read stories in their second language. • They then produce story maps to share with an "expert" group.	9:00–9:15 *Buddy Reading* Students read their Spanish language book to one Spanish-speaking student.
9:15–9:30 *Summary* Students write summaries of the English language story in Spanish.	**Thursday** *Buddy Interviews* Spanish and English language learners interview one another and then write reports in their second language based on their findings.	9:15–9:30 *Summary* Students write summaries of the Spanish language story in English.
9:30–10:15 *Major Dual Language Activity* (see inset)	**Friday** *Shared Writing* • Spanish and English language learners partner to write a story in either language. • Criteria: A beginning, middle, and end to the story, and proper punctuation.	9:30–10:15 *Major Dual Language Activity* (see inset)
10:15–10:35 *Literature* The teacher reads a story orally to the class, alternating languages daily, and asks comprehension questions.		10:15–10:35 *Literature* The teacher reads a story orally to the class, alternating languages daily, and asks comprehension questions.
To accommodate both classes during dual language instruction, the major activity can be scheduled at different times so that materials can be shared.		

Dual Language Instruction, Language Arts, Third Grade, Daily Plan For One Week

FIGURE **6**

——————————————— (Title)

(Body)

Paragraph Frame

Materials Scaffolds

Materials scaffolds, such as paragraph frames and story maps, also enabled students to eventually produce well-developed stories and expository texts independent of prompts. Students completed story maps and frames, which provided visual representations of the text, first in the first language and then in the second language.

Similarly, personal dictionaries developed by the students were used to record key vocabulary items in English and Spanish. For example, if students encountered an unfamiliar word during dual language instruction free reading, they added the word to their student dictionaries with an illustration, description, or definition. Following reading, the teacher provided time for both the English and Spanish language speakers to become "experts" for the second language learners. Experts helped novices complete new dictionary entries. In this way, personal dictionaries served as tools that the students could refer to when transferring concepts from one language to the other.

Additionally, wordless picture books provided an impetus for students to create developmentally appropriate stories in either their first or second language. Pictures helped students develop story lines. Working with a peer expert in the language used further supported students' language development and promoted the kinds of interpersonal relationships that have been associated with success for English language learners with and without disabilities (Ruiz et al., 1996).

Finally, the writing process (Ruiz et al., 1996), when routinely practiced in the students' first language, enabled them to then produce coherent written products in their second language, as predicted by theory (Collier, 1995b; Cummins, 1994a). In dual language instruction, second language learners worked with native speakers who provided guidance and support. Thus, native English speakers served as experts for English language learners. The roles were reversed when students wrote in Spanish. Students provided sophisticated literacy and language development scaffolds for one another during cognitively challenging academic tasks (Jiménez & Gersten, 1999; Tharp et al., 2000).

Task Scaffolds
While the reading and writing centers generally required adult help, the spelling and listening/art/creative expression centers were designed so that students could support one another. Instructions at these centers were typically illustrated or recorded. In other words, comprehensible information was embedded in the task so that students were able to complete them successfully.

Comprehensible Input Scaffolds
This type of scaffolding strategy was used in the dual language instruction phase, when students relied on their understanding of a scaffold in their first language as a tool to help them complete a similar task in their second language. For example, when English language learners with learning disabilities wrote letters in English, having mastered the letter form in Spanish, they were able to transfer the structural parts of a letter (e.g., heading, date, greeting, body, and closing) that they had learned in Spanish to writing a letter in English.

Effective Pedagogy in Action

Lena and Marta also put into practice the five guiding principles for effective pedagogy.

Work Collaboratively With Students/Create a Community of Learners

On a typical day during first language instruction, the students came in, sat down, and immediately turned their attention to the communication boards around the room. The boards assigned them to culturally and linguistically diverse cooperative learning groups where different tasks were to be completed. Each learning area was called a center, and cooperative learning groups were assigned to different centers that rotated throughout the course of the week. The front board listed the agenda for the day along with criteria for evaluating each center, the side board outlined a particular center or mini-lesson, and the back board told students which centers they would be attending that day. The teacher then greeted the class and reviewed student expectations. Students were chosen randomly to read and clarify the information on the communication boards. To set the stage for the first activity, the teacher focused on the literature selection, which was the theme for all of the centers. If a mini-lesson was needed to follow up on the previous day's center work, the teacher presented it in place of the literature activity.

These activities were designed to create a learning community in which students' prior knowledge about the reading selection was elicited and tied to their cultural realities before they moved to their centers. As the teacher and students developed a joint understanding of the literature, other adults in the room (who later facilitated the work at the centers) added their perceptions while they prepared their centers. Lena and Marta were fortunate in that they had several adults who acted as facilitators during language arts. They gathered materials, noted who would be attending their centers, and planned for appropriate student accommodations.

The work at the centers generally lasted from 45 minutes to 1 hour and was based on literature that was being read by the whole class. In the example provided in Figure 4, the story *Bringing the Rain to Kapiti Plain* was the literature piece that tied the work of the centers together. Following a mini-lesson or discussion of the literature, students moved to their centers.

Develop Language and Literacy Across the Curriculum/ Use Multiple Techniques to Promote Second Language Acquisition

Through the use of centers that focused on spelling, reading, writing, and creative expression during first language instruction, Lena and Marta were able to enhance learning across the language arts curriculum. For the English language learners with learning disabilities, this was especially important because these students are often relegated to "skill and drill" tasks, which tend to have a reductionist orientation (Ruiz & Figueroa, 1995).

During dual language instruction, the teachers found that language development and literacy were anchored by several major activities (see Figure 5), including wordless texts, literature circles, and shared writing. The multiple techniques that supported language acquisition for both English and Spanish language learners were personal dictionaries, buddy reading, and story summaries.

Connect School to Students' Lives/Incorporate Cultural Diversity Into Instruction

Before every language arts session during first language instruction, the teachers took time to connect the literature being studied to their students' cultures. For example, *Bringing the Rain to Kapiti Plain* featured a drought in an African desert. With their teachers, the students discussed how the desert they now lived in was like the desert in Africa and how they felt when it had not rained for a long time. They discussed how a drought affected their families, the animals in the desert, and their city.

Several of the major activities were student generated and student centered. For example, as part of the writing process, students wrote their own books, based on their experiences and interests. They then typed the words, drew illustrations, and bound and "published" their books. The products of their efforts naturally incorporated diversity into the curriculum and culturally relevant tasks into student work.

Teach Complex Thinking/Engage in Cognitively Challenging Activities

During first language instruction, each center accommodated both gifted students and those with learning disabilities. In addition, during whole-group mini-lesson time, Lena and Marta provided opportunities for students to synthesize, analyze, and problem solve. For example, students used analytical skills when they looked up words in dictionaries, identifying prefixes and suffixes and discovering multiple meanings.

During dual language instruction, for every activity that students completed in their second language, they demonstrated complex thinking. For example, a group of English language learners wrote a story with a beginning, middle, and ending in English, with help from their English-speaking peers. This activity prompted practical discussions about the production of stories and cognitively challenging metalinguistic discussions about ways to express ideas in the two languages.

Teach Through Conversation/Foster Extended Discourse

In each center group, conversations filled the air. In teacher-mediated centers, such as the reading and writing groups, the conversations were more deliberate as students discussed stories they had read, answering who, what, where, when, how, and why questions, with particular emphasis on the how and why. Additionally, in spelling and creative expression centers, students were encouraged to work with one another, discussing their strategies for learning.

Conversation during dual language instruction took place in both Spanish and English. <u>Many times one language was used to clarify meaning in the other.</u> Literature circles of mixed language groupings were the most intriguing occasion for extended discourse. When story maps and posters were presented to the whole group, discussions took place in Spanish and English, with students debating the problem of the story, the setting, and the main characters.

Classroom Implications
Scaffolding Strategies

Student work and teachers' records suggest that scaffolding strategies helped English language learners with learning disabilities to learn language arts content in their first language, Spanish, and then to carry out similar tasks in English. When given opportunities to develop proficiency in a task in their first language, they appeared to transfer what they had learned to their second language and to successfully complete the tasks with similar proficiency (Jiménez, García, & Pearson, 1996). In addition, English language learners with learning disabilities enjoyed substantial success in their roles as peer experts when working with Spanish language learners.

Principles for Effective Pedagogy

Lena and Marta's classroom experiences show that the five guiding principles for effective pedagogy can be applied to all learners regardless of ethnic background, geographic location, or disability (Collier, 1995b; Gersten & Jiménez, 1998; Tharp, Dalton, & Yamauchi, 1994; Tharp et al., 2000). First, the learning activities facilitated by the teachers were collaborative, whether the expert/novice interactions involved teacher/student, adult/student, or student/student groups. Second, the activities afforded multiple opportunities for learners to use both languages in appropriate ways. Third, learning was highly contextualized and culturally meaningful for the students in that the activities drew from their prior knowledge whenever possible. Fourth, students worked with a curriculum that was cognitively challenging and within their own personal zones of proximal development. Fifth, because of the variety of groupings for the different center activities, students were highly engaged through purposeful, goal-oriented dialogue and instructional conversations.

Dual Language Instruction

The data in the students' portfolios and teachers' records indicate that students benefited from working in their second language. In a supportive environment, students learning Spanish as their second language and those learning English as their second language actively participated in learning and took multiple risks in their work. During the second language activities, students with learning disabilities appeared to perform similarly to other learners. Behavior problems were minimal. The teachers and other adults in the room noted the respect that students showed for one another as they worked to achieve cognitively challenging tasks in their second language. Buddy reading took on a new meaning when students reading in their second language relied on a peer proficient in that language to assist with the decoding and pronunciation of words.

The affective benefits of dual language instruction appeared substantial. For example, when a native Spanish speaker with a learning disability was suddenly valued by his English-speaking peers as an expert in their second language, he became more engaged. Another Spanish speaker, who was receiving special education services in English, appeared to flourish when given the opportunity to work in her first language. While her writing in English was difficult for the LD resource teacher to comprehend, she was able to form coherent and complete sentences in Spanish. The implication was that this student needed to be reevaluated in both Spanish and English for placement in more appropriate special education or other academic programs. It is not uncommon for schools to confuse lack of proficiency in English with a learning disability (see Ortiz, this volume; Reyes & Bos, 1996). In this case, dual language instruction provided valuable information to both the general and special educator while appearing to boost the self-confidence of the learner.

Conclusion

In reflecting on their classroom experiences with scaffolding strategies and dual language instruction, Lena and Marta noted that this instruction was not without challenge and difficulty. Both teachers commented that the planning time they had was not adequate. They also found it difficult to locate the same or similar materials in English and Spanish. They found that some of the students who were regrouped for dual language instruction struggled. It took them a week or more to adjust to the change in the classroom composition and procedures.

Despite these challenges, both teachers firmly concluded that scaffolding strategies and dual language instruction held tremendous promise with English language learners with learning disabilities. Marta and Lena felt that first language instruction prior to dual language instruction was crucial, as it provided students with valuable tools and strategies that they were able to transfer to their second languages. Lena and Marta's experiences show how committed teachers who are willing to take risks can accomplish real educational change for English language learners with learning disabilities.

Walking the Talk: The Joys and Challenges of Critical Pedagogy

Barbara S. C. Goldstein, *Azusa Pacific University*

Originally developed in the context of nonformal adult education, the work of Paulo Freire (1970, 1973, 1985) in critical pedagogy has been applied to higher education (Geismar & Nicoleau, 1993) and, to some extent, secondary school education (Diaz-Greenberg, 1997; McLaren, 1994). Elementary-level classroom teachers and special educators have also discovered that critical pedagogy may enhance the educational experiences of students and teachers (Goldstein, 1995; Rúiz & Enguidanos, 1997). Efforts to apply this approach in the education of students with special needs have gained some attention in the literature (de Valenzuela, Connery, & Musanti, 2000; Sanchez, 1999; Thousand et al., 1999). This chapter explores the application of Freire's work to the education of English language learners with special needs and shows how teachers who work with these students have put his educational philosophy into practice.

The Context: Back to Basics and Proposition 227

Reading instruction, special education, and bilingual education have been the focus of reform efforts nationwide. In California, changes in policies and instructional trends have directly affected the educational environment for English language learners with special needs. In language and literacy instruction, two major state policy changes are the move from a whole language approach to reading to a phonics-based approach, and the passage of Proposition 227, an initiative that essentially did away with bilingual education in California.

The move to a phonics-based approach to reading was ignited by dismal statewide scores in reading. A focus on literature rather than controlled readers, and an emphasis on the writing process rather than on accuracy, gave further impetus to voters' fears about the lack of direct instruction in spelling, phonics, and correction. Low state test scores led to the appointment of a new state board of education whose members promoted back-to-basics approaches that emphasized phonics, decoding, phonemic awareness, spelling, and explicit skills instruction. Concerns that teachers who had been schooled in whole language approaches did not know how to teach phonics led to a proliferation of reading programs prescribing highly structured, step-by-step instructions that teachers were required to follow.

Highly structured curricula are not unknown to special educators; in fact, they are often used in self-contained classrooms instead of the core curricula offered to general education students. In bilingual (Spanish and English) general education and bilingual special education classes, however, literature-based, process-oriented instruction with meaningful and authentic reading and writing activities were showing great promise for English language learners who had not mastered the sounds of English and who were developing English vocabulary (Rúiz, 1989, 1995a, 1995b; Rúiz & Enguidanos, 1997). This approach did not ignore skills instruction (including phonics and phonemic awareness) but rather presented it within a context of meaningful content (see, for example, Snow, Burns, & Griffin, 1998).

Teachers had the leeway to determine when a student was experiencing difficulties and to decide how to intervene. Mini-lessons consisting of instruction in specific skills were developed with individual student strengths and needs in mind. First language instruction or support was provided as needed.

The passage of Proposition 227 did not eradicate native language instruction or support for English language learners eligible for special education services under federal law, but it did reduce opportunities for first language instruction and support (Rueda, Artiles, Salazar, & Higareda, in press). The movement away from first language support is especially worrisome given two other recent developments in special education: the overrepresentation of Spanish-speaking English language learners in special education classes and the growing support among special educators for the inclusion of students with mild to moderate learning disabilities in general education classes.

While those who advocate inclusion debate the nature and course of inclusive practices with those who advocate a continuum of special education services, English language learners with special needs continue to sit in self-contained classes taught only in English with no native language support and with highly structured curricula and repetitive activities. The current reforms mean that more English language learners will be subjected to these educational practices in their general education classes.

Critical Pedagogy: A Radical Approach

In critical pedagogy, "the teacher creates the conditions in the classroom for students to become empowered by becoming aware of the presence of knowledge and power in their own lives that oppress and liberate" (Goldstein, 1996b, p. 32). This approach to teaching, and specifically to reading, uses the students' knowledge and experiences as the context for the development of vocabulary, content knowledge, oral language skills, and writing. In problem posing, a major feature of critical pedagogy, the teacher poses open-ended questions regarding real-life problems for students to reflect on, discuss, and redefine.

Through a process of dialogue, reflection, and action, the Freirean approach to literacy instruction seeks to transform policies, practices, laws, and structures that contribute to illiteracy and social, economic, and political oppression and disempowerment. In contrast to the banking model of education, in which the teacher deposits knowledge into the heads of students to be withdrawn later during a test, the Freirean approach creates a community of learners in which teachers and students enter into a dialogue. The dialogue produces themes, vocabulary, and ideas based on student concerns and interests that in turn become the basis for the curriculum. Proposed actions that evolve from the discussions are critiqued and examined, and the ensuing literacy activities are based on real situations that students must face. (For a brief summary of Freire's approach to literacy, see Spener, 1992; for a more thorough description of critical pedagogy, see Freire's *Pedagogy of the Oppressed,* 1970.)

Special educators, particularly those whose work has focused on bilingual students with special needs, have been quick to recognize the need for radical change in how students are identified and served in special and general education. Critical pedagogy does not advocate specific changes in student placement or evaluation. However, a teacher who understands the philosophical, economic, historical, and sociological foundations on which a special education program, assessment tool, or curriculum has evolved is more likely to begin a dialogue with students, parents, administrators, and other teachers about the implications of and the assumptions behind these practices. Instructional practices may subsequently emerge that reflect the goals of the community and that are congruent with critical pedagogy as a life-changing educational experience.

Researchers have explored the development of the critical pedagogical teacher (Frank, 1993; Giroux, 1988) and classroom practices that have been successful in special education classes with bilingual students (Ruiz, 1989). Darder (1991) provides a theoretical foundation for teachers who embrace a philosophy of critical pedagogy for bicultural education. This theory describes the relationship between culture and power in educational institutions. These teachers

> deliberately organize against isolation, make student and adult alliances whenever possible, build multiracial/multicultural alliances, actively oppose all 'isms,' examine personal practice, commit to social justice and peace, oppose classroom practices that undermine the rights of children of color, hold high expectations for all students, and strive to promote a child-centered curriculum. (Thousand et al, 1999, p. 324)

My own work with teachers who strive to enact critical pedagogy on a daily basis convinces me that the above description of what critical pedagogical teachers do is often an ideal goal rather than the current reality.

To be a critical educator is an ongoing struggle. It is a struggle to maintain a heightened awareness of one's own biases and assumptions and then examine how these assumptions influence practice. It is a struggle to create an educational environment that seeks to make relationships of power and privilege explicit and understandable to students and their families. It is a struggle to work within a system that has often supported practices that contribute to the miseducation of the working poor and children of color. Teachers who practice critical pedagogy also endeavor to provide educational experiences that will bring meaningful context to language and literacy instruction, English language development, math and science instruction, and arts and physical education instruction.

Special Education and Critical Pedagogy

My own work in a first-, second-, and third-grade self-contained special education classroom designed for Spanish-speaking English language learners with learning disabilities demonstrated that Freire's "pedagogy of the oppressed" (Freire, 1970) was truly applicable. My students experienced oppression because of economic poverty that limited their access to adequate housing, medical care, and social and political voice. They experienced discriminatory practices based on their skin color and language. They struggled with language development. They had also internalized negative images of themselves as "bad," "dumb," and *"malito"* ('sick') because of their diffculties with language and communication. Their efforts to fit in were thwarted by their history of repeated failure as much as by their so-called disabilities.

The challenge for me was to combine Freire's pedagogy with best practices for English language learners who were also Spanish-speaking students from poor working families. Baca and Cervantes' (1984) seminal work on bilingual special education, and the research of Langdon (1989), Moll (1990), Ortiz (1984, 1991), Rueda (1984, 1989, 1993), Rueda and Goldman (1988), and Rúiz (1989, 1995a, 1995b) provided the framework to address the language and learning difficulties that my students brought to the classroom. Bilingual special education is a field of study that examines the needs of students with mild, moderate, and severe disabilities, who have a primary language other than English, and who are learning English. These students have varying degrees of proficiency in their native language and in English, ranging from virtually no speaking proficiency in either language to oral fluency in both languages but with limited reading and writing skills. (See Valdés and Figueroa, 1994, for a description of different types of bilingualism.)

Although bilingual special education includes students with first languages other than Spanish, researchers have focused primarily on Spanish-speaking students whose proficiency in English is limited. The parents of these students historically have been denied access to knowledge regarding special education services and educational rights for their children who have been identified as disabled. Most importantly, students identified, or misidentified, as disabled and placed in special education programs with no native language support have made limited progress (Wilkinson & Ortiz, 1986). The English language learners in my self-contained class could be described as having limited skills in English and increasingly limited skills in Spanish.

It was not difficult to integrate Freire's work with the best practices that bilingual special educators were advocating. The learner-centered approaches proposed by special educators fit in with Freire's view that education should revolve around students' lives and that its purpose is to help learners become aware of the forces at work in their daily lives. Problem posing allows students to unravel the complexities of their social and political realities. The students in my self-contained classroom could benefit from children's literature that contained topics related to their own experiences. They could be encouraged to explore those topics and to tell their own stories.

A critical pedagogical approach does not ignore the specific skills that students with learning differences need. Rather, it reframes how those skills are presented and assessed (Goldstein, 1996b). Echevarría (1995), Goldstein (1996b), and Ruiz (1989) found that specific skills related to decoding, writing, spelling, and math could be explicitly taught within mini-lessons tailored to the needs of the students. Furthermore, these mini-lessons could be embedded in students' writing, dictation, and literature-based vocabulary activities.

Using a critical pedagogical approach with English language learners with special needs requires an examination of the students' language abilities since dialogue with peers and teachers is crucial to problem posing. For my students, the use of cloze sentences (in which students fill in words in blank spaces) enabled them to share their understandings of and reactions to the readings and discussions and provided them with a framework on which to build their own sentences. Through repetition of oral and written sentence structures, student illustrations of vocabulary definitions, and story comprehension questions, my students developed the beginning tools they needed to build and benefit from a problem-posing approach.

The Critical Pedagogy of Two Teachers

Over the past 5 years, I have had the opportunity to work closely with critical educators in the public school system. We have explored issues of social justice, critical theory in education, and transformative education. My discussions with these teachers form the basis for much of this chapter. My purpose has been to explore the ways in which these teachers continue to hold fast to their commitment to liberatory educational practices in the face of formidable challenges. I have also attempted to discover classroom practices that are common to teachers who use critical pedagogical approaches in their instruction.

Two individuals exemplify the varied experiences of these teachers. One teaches in an English immersion classroom, and the other teaches in a classroom that provides first language instruction for Spanish speakers. By examining their experiences and practice, we can better understand those elements that transform classrooms into communities of learners, similar to Freire's *culture circles,* or liberation theology's *comunidades de base,* where students engage in problem-posing discussions and activities to discover the historical, cultural, economic, and sociopolitical forces that have brought them to this time and place in their lives.

Lisa: Third-Grade Teacher

Lisa is a third-grade teacher in a class for English language learners. Long before she became a teacher, Lisa was interested in working for social justice. Her experiences in college courses as an undergraduate and a graduate student strengthened her belief in social justice theory and application.

Teaching Style

Lisa strives to create an environment in which students learn not only to read and write but also to develop, share, and write about those events in their lives that are meaningful to them. "What kids have to say is worthy of telling," Lisa says. "They have enough in them to come up with their own pieces of work. Their life has meaning, and it is rich. They don't need a writing prompt."

Lisa's Latino and African American students explore second language issues in classroom discussions of themes from poems they study and problems that characters face in the books they read. For example, Lisa led discussions with her class on the impact of Proposition 227, the law that effectively ended bilingual education in California in 1998. Her students discussed the impact of the law on her ability to make decisions about her teaching and on their ability to engage in first language activities and use certain materials in class. They examined the law's far-reaching impact on their lives—how it affected the role of their native language in the school and their sense of identity and self-respect. The third graders in Lisa's class were not strangers to language issues, as most of them were either Spanish-speaking English language learners or African American students growing up in a bilingual (Spanish and English) neighborhood. They understood, commensurate with their cognitive development, the dynamics of language and culture and the issues of status and power at work in the school and the society at large.

Curriculum and Learning Activities

Balancing the required curriculum with a teacher- and student-created curriculum is a struggle for Lisa. "I didn't get a masters to be told how to teach and to just teach without thinking," she says. What to present from the scripted teacher guides and curriculum, what to pursue from the students' ideas, and how to integrate these are daily decisions that Lisa must make. "I don't use teacher guides exactly as they're pre-scribed. I look at the material in the book and decide how to teach it," Lisa explains.

In Lisa's classroom, students participate in discussions about social and community issues. In their discussions of Proposition 227, Lisa introduced books that illustrated the dilemma regarding language use and the language of instruction. She then created opportunities for oral reading and writers workshop sessions, in which students developed individual or group-written pieces that were revised, published, and shared. "Kids are excited about reading and writing," Lisa says. "Even the lowest kids experience success. I get really good stories from one of my lowest kids. She loves to write because she realizes she has good stories to tell."

For students like this, Lisa creates multilevel group projects so students can make valuable contributions and be recognized by peers for their strengths. This student had reading and writing difficulties, yet she continued to write independently. She had strong oral language skills and excellent storytelling abilities that demonstrated a well-developed sense of story and narrative skills. She also demonstrated keen and sophisticated observations during discussions and participated in the peer revision and editing sessions of the writers workshop.

"What's amazing to me about writers workshop is that even students who are 'low' love writing," Lisa notes. Students choose their own topics and edit their writing; share their writing with each other; and give each other feedback on the topics, content, organization, and other aspects of the work. Students choose whether or not to publish their work. Publishing may include illustrating, typing, and binding the book pages (Graves, 1983).

During these and other activities, the language and literacy needs of students with special education needs are not ignored. Lisa addresses these specific needs through mini-conferences, readers theater (in which students create a script from narrative text and perform it for an audience), and individual activities designed to meet individual learning needs. The mini-conferences (brief one-to-one student-teacher conferences) include opportunities for students to evaluate their own work with teacher guidance. During this time, students analyze their work samples, choose samples for their portfolios (self-selected samples of work that demonstrate growth over time), set instructional goals for specific areas, and plan activities to reach those goals. Mini-conferences may include specific skills instruction as well. In addition, Lisa creates individualized mini-lessons, brief one-to-one or small-group lessons that address the specific skills that an individual student or a small group needs.

Working Against a Recipe Approach to Teaching

One of Lisa's personal struggles as a critical teacher is to provide her students with the knowledge and skills they will need to succeed in other classes, where the way of doing things may be very different from her own approach and instruction much more structured and fixed, regardless of where students are in their development. Just because teachers use terms such as *literature based, writers workshop,* and *mini-lessons* does not mean that they understand the underlying theoretical and philosophical notions that support these methods and carry them out. In many classes, these ideas have been reduced to a technique that is devoid of social and philosophical intent and that has been packaged to sell as reproducible classroom activities. Students' voices are silenced in the making of educational cookbooks whose recipes are to be followed in any context with any group of students, regardless of their circumstances and experiences.

Creating an Inclusive Environment

Lisa's class structure and instructional style attempt to meet the needs of the diverse learners in her class, including those with special needs. "I don't think fairness means that everyone gets the same but that everyone gets what they need," says Lisa, who supports inclusion and believes that her classroom would be a good setting for students with special needs provided that she also receives support and training. One form of support that Lisa favors is the assistance of an aide trained to work with children with special needs. She and the aide would need adequate time to plan together. The aide would need to learn how to conduct mini-conferences, and she and the aide would need to agree on teaching approaches and classroom management philosophies. Lisa believes that team teaching is more successful if teachers share similar philosophies.

Parent Involvement

Providing parents an active role in the formal education of their children is a critical component of Lisa's teaching. She invites parents to come to the classroom, contribute their stories and abilities, and participate in their children's projects. My observations of Lisa's interactions with parents shows a teacher who is genuine and respectful of other cultures. She attempts to help parents discover their strengths and see how these might be used to enhance their children's formal educational experiences. She does not attempt to teach parents how to teach their children; rather, she creates opportunities for parents to become involved in the classroom so that they may begin to feel that the school is an institution that should serve *their* interests and goals.

Surviving the Challenges

As a child, Lisa did not always like school, although she excelled academically. She tries to teach how she wishes that she had been taught. Lisa's religious faith is a source of strength and guidance as she observes what happens in her class. Her faith keeps her from feeling overwhelmed as she struggles to practice critical pedagogy. Opportunities for self-reflection abound as she works toward national board certification, mentors new teachers, and teaches a science class that serves as a model classroom for improving science education. Yet she continues to feel that there are times when she has to teach in a way that is inconsistent with national trends toward teaching for standardized tests, drilling and testing skills-based activities, and using scripted curricula.

Lisa recommends that new teachers develop a long-term vision for growing into critical pedagogy. "Read professional literature, observe other teachers, think about what you do, and take time to analyze what you're doing and why. Know the reason. Do what you know is best for the students."

Guadalupe: K–1 Teacher

Guadalupe is a K–1 teacher in a classroom for English language learners, most of whom speak Spanish. Her class is designated to provide first language instruction as needed to help the children. How primary language instructional support is defined, however, is a question at Guadalupe's school.

Guadalupe's own journey to critical education began in high school when an inspiring teacher took the time to help her learn English so that she could pass the examinations for high school graduation. He encouraged her to continue her education so that she could also make a contribution to her community. Guadalupe has worked for community agencies and schools for 18 years.

Teaching Style

Guadalupe's instructional approach is built on respect for the hearts and minds of children. She determines what they know about a subject; tries to find out what is important to them; and creates opportunities for them to discover and discuss new ideas, read materials on related topics to gain more information, and connect the ideas to their own lives. "I can't say that I will teach the same thing to all of them," Guadalupe says. "I'm going to teach a given subject, but it doesn't mean the same thing to all of them. We have to teach what the children need and want. We work from where they are. Everything has to be related to their own experiences."

Guadalupe's interaction with students is characterized by questions that lead them to analyze their own thinking and then guide them to the next level of questions. "I ask them what they know," Guadalupe says. "When we find problems, we try to find what is possible. What can we do to move on to the next step? What do they need to know? If they tell me it doesn't make sense, we ask more questions."This type of Socratic questioning permeates all of the subjects covered in Guadalupe's class, including math, science, social studies, and language.

First Language Support

The language of instruction is a key issue in Guadalupe's class. According to California's bilingual/English language development program, her Spanish-speaking students should receive about 20% of their instruction in Spanish. Unfortunately, the school administration does not support even that limited amount. The school considers the Spanish used at recess and lunch to make up the requisite 20%, which means that in the classroom only English can be used. Guadalupe's concerns about the restrictions on first language use in the classroom, and her questions about the highly structured English reading program, have been met with indifference, hostility, and amusement by administrators and some fellow teachers. Those teachers who share her concerns have chosen to remain silent. Some offer their support in private but continue to adhere to the instructional boundaries. Like so many other teachers who practice critical education, Guadalupe teaches her students in Spanish when they need it to understand. At the same time, she helps them develop their English skills so that they can move on and do well in their other classes.

Creating an Inclusive Environment

Guadalupe feels that her classroom structure provides an environment that is conducive to learning for all students, including those with special needs. The students work on group projects, discuss their instructional options and activities, learn in different centers, and discuss their work with one another. They have choices about what and how they learn: They choose topics and materials that they need for completing projects, discuss what the next steps are, and determine what the goals and evaluation benchmarks will be. Guadalupe provides questions and guidance to help them come up with answers and *caminos* ('pathways') that meet their educational, practical, social, and political needs.

Guadalupe believes that when children have options and experiences to discuss and work with, they will learn. They don't all have to be doing the same thing at the same time. She says, "They have to see things for themselves. They have to explore." She allows them to make mistakes; they have to experience things for themselves or they won't know what happened, she explains. "Then you give them the steps and show them how to do it. *Se tienen que caer para saber como levantarse* ('They have to fall down to learn how to get up')."

A simple incident illustrates the value of the problem-posing and mediational approach in teaching and learning. Once, during one of my visits to Guadalupe's class, the student who was in charge of the plants spilled a bucket of water on the floor and asked Guadalupe what to do. Students have responsibility for the organization and care of the classroom, so instead of telling the student to clean the floor, pick up the bucket, and next time not fill it to the top, Guadalupe asked the student questions so that he could come up with suitable solutions himself. The interaction took longer than it would have taken to tell the child what to do, but these interactions provide opportunities for students to develop an awareness of themselves as thinkers who can come up with their own action plans and solutions.

Guadalupe believes that this experiential approach (which I would describe as mediated learning experiences within the zone of proximal development) is how we all learn. Children with special needs also benefit from this type of interaction, but they may require more explicit instruction and more intense guidance for longer periods of time.

Obstacle to an Inclusive Environment
An obstacle to creating an inclusive environment for English language learners with special needs is the school district's adherence to the required curriculum. The reading program is highly scripted and timed. Guadalupe describes it as including "drills for five minutes, then a timer rings and you go to the next activity, and so forth." The schedule has no flexibility for teachers to make instructional decisions that vary from the prescribed program. Consequently, students with special needs, or those not identified as having special needs but who are struggling, are left further and further behind. "It's not success for all if it's treating all kids the same," Guadalupe says. "Provide accommodations. Don't keep moving if they don't get it. Treating them the same isn't giving them what they need."

Guadalupe has voiced her concerns, often and loudly. Unfortunately, she feels her concerns are largely ignored and that she has been branded a troublemaker. "I tell [the program administrators], 'I want to do this right. I want [the students] to learn how to read and write. If I'm not doing it the right way, show me.' They tell me, 'Do this.' I tell them my concerns about that and why it's not working. I ask them, 'How can we make it better so it works right?' and they don't say anything." To teach in a way that is consistent with her beliefs, Guadalupe does what she has to do, even if that means closing the door to her classroom.

She believes that teaching the prescribed curriculum as presented by the publishers of the reading program would be tantamount to deliberately miseducating her students. By not providing each child with the type of educational practice crucial to student learning—with opportunities for students to examine, discuss, and reflect on their life experiences—critical teachers may feel that they are contributing to the continued subordinated status of their students and their students' communities.

Guadalupe feels that one of the key problems is that teachers are not trusted to change educational environments and policies, and students are not trusted to do their own learning. Therefore, teachers are told what to do; students are told what to learn and how to learn it; and the way to make sure everyone is doing what they are told is to test, test, and test.

A Sense of Isolation and Time to Heal

By closing her classroom door, Guadalupe exacerbates the isolation that she already feels. For Guadalupe, and for many critical teachers, isolation is a key issue. There is only one other person in the school with whom Guadalupe can share ideas comfortably and who understands her perspective. "Many times I feel like I'm drowning," she says.

At this point in her career, Guadalupe feels she must soon leave her classroom to regain her health and perspective. Burnout, fatigue, loss of energy, and a feeling of overwhelming isolation are common for teachers attempting to work in systems that are at odds with their per-

sonal and professional values of equity, excellence, respect fo
social justice, and integrity. Guadalupe will not leave education
ing entirely but will return to the community educational progra
she helped create.

For Guadalupe, the hard part is leaving the students. "They question
me, and it's okay," she says. "I want them to tell me what they think
and feel. They provide honest feedback." Guadalupe values their hon-
esty. It allows her to respond to their concerns, and her responsiveness
gives them the power of their voice.

Elements of Critical Pedagogy

Lisa's and Guadalupe's teaching is consistent with best practices for
English language learners. These practices have also been identified as
best practices for English language learners with mild to moderate
learning difficulties. They include writers workshop (Rúiz, 1989), dialogue journals (Rueda & Goldman, 1988), literature-based reading
activities (Ortiz, 1991), mini-lessons tailored to the needs of individual
learners, and project-based instruction (Goldstein, 1996a). Because
their educational environments offer a variety of activities and choices,
students with special needs are readily accepted and integrated into
their classes and programs. Accommodations are built into the basic
design and need only be fine-tuned for individual students. Even students with moderate to severe learning difficulties can be adequately
served with additional classroom support.

Both Lisa and Guadalupe use a variety of instructional techniques to
develop their students' metacognitive capacities and their awareness of
being partners in the learning process. Mediated learning experiences
(Feuerstein, 1979) and mediating questions encourage the students to
examine their own thinking and to develop complex classification and
logical reasoning strategies for problem solving. This instructional dialogue occurs within a Vygotskian (1978) model in which the teacher
guides the student and intervenes when necessary with essential information, questions, and feedback (Tharp & Gallimore, 1988).

Question-and-answer periods evolve into instructional conversations (Echevarría, 1995) and lead to an emergent curriculum based on student interests and experiences (Goldstein, 1996a). Through the use of language charts (Ortiz, 1991), Guadalupe and Lisa facilitate conversations that link instruction to their students' lives. Posted on the classroom wall, the language chart typically includes the title of a text the students have read, the author's name, and a series of questions or prompts. After recording the students' responses to the questions and prompts, the teacher then leads the students in a discussion connecting their responses to their personal experiences (Goldstein, 1995).

Lisa and Guadalupe also provide their students with choices. Their classrooms contain different mini-educational spaces: a library, comfortable reading areas, listening centers, math centers, and a small-group work center for specific skills instruction or teacher-student conferences.

Finally, both teachers use assessment to inform the direction that their teaching will take. Assessment is specifically geared toward improving teaching: It naturally occurs in the course of the day, it is based on classroom instruction, and it views students' errors as opportunities to analyze their understanding of the instruction. Assessment informs the explicit and individualized small-group mini-lessons that both teachers regularly employ. Learning records (Barr, 1997), reading records (Clay, 1985), work samples, and interactive journals (Rueda & Goldman, 1988) are examples of assessment materials used. (See Figure 1 for a list of instructional practices used by Lisa and Guadalupe and other critical educators.)

Discussion

By examining the themes that emerge from the work of these two critical educators, we can begin to identify those practices that promote a viable and transformative educational experience for all students. Seven practices in particular stand out:

- Interactive, student-centered instruction
- Student-centered behavior management
- Mediational questioning
- Multilevel activities
- Emergent curriculum: connecting personal experience to community and global issues
- Collaboration with parents and the community
- Surviving with integrity and hope

GURE **1** ■

- Literature-based reading curriculum
- Writers workshop
- Language experience approach
- Dialogue journals
- Instructional conversations
- Reciprocal reading and conversations
- Mediated learning experiences
- Centers and choices
- Multimodal instruction
- Discovery and hands-on learning
- Mini-lessons for explicit skills-based instruction as needed
- Language charts
- Culturally and linguistically affirming instructional materials and classroom environment
- Emergent curriculum (as opposed to scripted curriculum)
- Student-generated topics for discussion, writing, and connections to reading
- Group projects and action research

Practices in Critical Pedagogy

Interactive, Student-Centered Instructional Practices

In classes taught by critical educators, students actively participate in their own learning. Opportunities are created for students to examine and explore ideas in collaborative group projects and action research. Students have opportunities to reflect on and share their work with others, a central practice in Freire's pedagogy, as critical awareness occurs within communities of learners as well as within individuals.

Teachers know that students who are engaged in interactive learning take responsibility for each other's learning. Action research (research directed toward social change) and projects that result in a product are completed in cooperative working groups, with everyone being invited to contribute to the group effort. Action research demands that students discuss their topic, formulate and decide upon their questions, identify their research sources, come up with an action plan, and divide the work. When students are reading a passage during a literature circle or doing research for a presentation, they use various reciprocal reading approaches (Palincsar & Brown, 1984, 1989), which require them to take active roles in the group's learning experience. Individual students take the roles of summarizer, clarifier, questioner, and predictor. Many teachers who use this approach to reading comprehension also have a student take the role of visualizer or artist. As students read a passage, they stop at intervals to summarize, clarify, question, predict, and visually encode what they have read.

Writers workshop is another interactive, student-centered activity that takes place on a regular basis. It is a continuous activity as students are at different stages in the composing, revising, and publishing cycle of their works. Writing topics come from the students' discussions of content area study, such as an emergent theme from a social studies chapter, their reaction to a literature book, or their own personal experience. Writers workshop prompts may also result from a critical incident in the classroom, such as the discovery by Guadalupe's students that their first language is forbidden in the class.

Ten Instructional Strategies of Critical Educators

- Use children's literature that explores social and cultural themes of interest to the students.

- Use students' retelling of the literature as texts for reading, spelling, and grammar lessons.

- Have students use art to create visualizations of key vocabulary or concepts.

- Encourage the use of students' personal stories as the basis for writers workshop activities.

- Provide students with models for questioning (e.g., What is another way to say that? What if…? When have you done something similar?) and for discussion.

- Design lessons around social and cultural themes that students have identified as of interest.

- Create opportunities for students to share community events, local news, or personal anecdotes. Morning circle time is often the best venue for this activity.

- Allow students to debrief at the end of the day in large or small groups. Post concerns that need to be addressed. If necessary, ask questions to guide the debriefing (e.g., Can you tell me one thing you learned today? What did you like best/least about the lesson/activity? How could we do it differently next time?).

- Help students identify and access resources for projects or research in which they are interested.

- Provide a model for analyzing action research projects through questioning (e.g., Who in the community can help us with this? What are some tools we will need to do this work? What will be the hardest thing for us to do in order to complete this project? What are some problems we might face? How will we evaluate our work when we are finished? How will we know when we are done?).

Student-Centered Behavior Management

Teachers know that students who are engaged in learning that is meaningful and interactive are less likely to be disruptive. Both Guadalupe and Lisa have virtually no classroom management problems with their students, even though both have students who had previously been considered by other teachers to have behavioral problems. Students identified as having special needs, especially those identified as learning disabled, often have a history of behavioral difficulties, yet the behavior of the special needs students in Lisa and Guadalupe's classes does not stand out.

In contrast to the traditional classroom in which the teacher is the sole arbiter of behavior, in the critical educator's classroom, students are actively involved in defining acceptable classroom behavior and setting the limits of tolerance and the consequences for students who are disruptive. Both Lisa and Guadalupe hold regular classroom meetings in which students are able to discuss events, problems, or questions regarding future classroom plans or outings. The combination of highly engaging interactive learning activities and student-centered standards for behavior makes it less likely that students with special needs will experience frustration and more likely that they will experience academic and social success.

Mediational Questioning for Critical Awareness

Feuerstein's (1979) work with students with developmental disabilities provides a model for questioning that can help teachers and students formulate questions designed to go beyond literal comprehension and examine underlying assumptions. Students typically are not encouraged to learn the skill of asking questions, especially those that challenge deeply held educational assumptions.

Teacher questions serve two main purposes. First, they provide a model for students to learn how to ask critical questions. Second, they help students develop metacognitive understanding of their own thinking process. Questions in a problem-posing classroom may guide students to further inquiry that leads them to a deeper understanding of both the subject under question and the nature of the critical inquiry process itself. For instance, when Guadalupe asks students what they need to do to solve a practical problem in the classroom, she is not only guiding them in their search for a solution, she is also teaching them to think about their thinking by getting them to use all of the information they have and apply this knowledge to the new situation.

For elementary school-aged students to develop an "awareness of awareness, of thinking about thinking, of interpreting our interpretations," (Berthoff, 1987, cited in Freire & Macedo, 1987, p. xi), questions serve as guideposts that can point them in the right direction. Teachers have to provide as much support as students need so that they can participate in the discussions and ask questions themselves, particularly if students are also English language learners with special needs. As Guadalupe tells us, we have to start where the students are.

Multilevel Activities

Guadalupe's and Lisa's emergent curricula take into account multiple learning abilities and styles. Diverse activities enable all students to participate and learn.

The physical structure of the classrooms does not reflect the traditional configuration—desks in rows with the teacher's desk at the front of the class. In the critical educator's classroom, there is no one center of learning but rather several focus areas throughout the room. These specialized areas, such as a writers workshop publishing center, may remain throughout the year. Other centers, such as a center for a particular science unit or action project, may be seasonal or thematic. It is clear that these classrooms provide a setting for multiple purposes and a wide range of activities. In smaller classrooms, seating arrangements are flexible and constantly changing, depending on the activity. Another physical characteristic of student-centered, multilevel classes is that materials are easily accessible to students.

The instructional activities, like the learning centers, reflect a variety of student learning styles, interests, and strengths. For instance, students may be responsible for different aspects of an action research project, thereby tapping into their individual strengths. One student may be the recorder, another the artist, another the speaker, and still another the media person. The students' roles may change continuously, with the group deciding how to implement the project and how to provide support for each other.

The multilevel activities enable the teacher to provide experiences that may be broad or deep in scope, depending on the student's particular challenges and gifts. Lisa's third graders may work on a multimedia presentation in which one student's learning objective is to identify and name related objects and to write and print those words, while another's is to write about how different concepts work together in an area of study.

In Guadalupe's class, students are engaged in hands-on activities. All students have opportunities to explore concepts and ideas in concrete projects, with different activities to meet different needs.

Emergent Curriculum: Community Concerns and Global Issues

Areas for further study emerge from the continuing dialogue among students and the teacher. In these dialogues, students often think and talk about the issue in question in light of their personal experience and then connect the issue to larger issues in the community. This in turn may lead to new action research projects and activities that will enhance students' understanding of the concerns they have identified. Their understanding may emerge from writing their own stories based on personal experience and then comparing these stories to published stories with similar themes. Curriculum topics and issues of interest can be examined in light of the students' own experiences in school and in the community. If the topic were the cutbacks in bilingual education, for example, students might interview relatives, community members, and teachers to discover themes and patterns relating to language use. Students might further explore the similarity between their community's experience of linguistic subordination and that of the deaf community.

Collaboration With Parents and the Community

Collaboration with parents and other community members helps bring the two worlds of school and home together. Different languages and cultures complicate this task, particularly for students who speak languages other than English and grapple with two languages and cultures, each with its own rules and expectations, in two distinct domains—school and the home and community.

Outreach to Spanish-speaking parents of students with special needs is particularly important because these parents are often not aware of the services and protections to which they and their children are entitled. (For a discussion of these rights and protections, see García, this volume.) Critical teachers look for ways to make parents feel comfortable within the classroom setting so that they may eventually understand that they are partners with the teachers in the education of their children. Because Lisa and Guadalupe live in the communities where they teach, they see students and parents outside of the school setting, which facilitates the relationships that they have with the parents. It is not necessary, however, to live in the community to establish trust and common concerns and interests with parents. When parents do not come to the school or classroom, critical teachers go to the parents— in their homes, churches, recreation centers, or meeting places—to begin the dialogue.

Surviving With Integrity and Hope

Critical teachers struggle to survive with integrity and hope. Because they see the connection between education, public policy, economics, global politics, and social justice, critical teachers are often involved in activities outside of their school hours. They are involved in church groups, community groups, and labor unions. They are active members of their schools and communities. They engage in formal and informal professional development. Figure 2 lists common characteristics of teachers who practice critical pedagogy.

Such additional commitments contribute a sense of community connection and support, but they may also contribute to physical fatigue. Worse is the spiritual fatigue that comes from trying to "walk the talk," to do what one knows is beneficial for the students' educational needs,

FIGURE **2** ■

Critical educators...

- link students' personal history and experiences to community issues;
- respect students as learners and respect their prior knowledge and experiences;
- respect students' ethnic and linguistic backgrounds;
- understand community expectations and concerns;
- strive for professional integrity;
- avoid labeling students and communities;
- take risks;
- do what must be done, even if it is unpopular;
- play an active role in community organizations;
- read and critique professional literature;
- work together with other teachers, parents, and members of the community;
- become aware of community resources;
- demonstrate critical consciousness in relation to self, students, instructional practices, and community and public policy issues;
- share information and speak up;
- welcome critique from other critically conscious educators and colleagues; and
- may feel isolated and overwhelmed.

Common Characteristics of Teachers who Practice Critical Pedagogy though it may be politically unpopular and in some cases detrimental to one's job security. Isolation exacerbates burnout. When there is no one at the school who understands the nature of critical pedagogy and liberatory educational practices, and when policies work against this type of instruction, teachers become isolated.

The current political climate regarding educational achievement has created a stance of resistance among critical educators to policies, trends, and practices that they see as counterproductive to the goals of social justice. Both Guadalupe and Lisa feel that they have to close the door to their classrooms to be effective teachers. The closed door can be viewed not only as symbolic of the isolation that teachers like Lisa and Guadalupe feel but also as a metaphor for the resistance to imposed policies. A closed door is not a solution. It not only reinforces teacher isolation that can lead to burnout, but it also limits the possibility of a genuine dialogue among educators that could lead to greater understanding of the social and political forces at work in educational policy and practice.

Figure 3 illustrates some of the obstacles to applying critical pedagogy in educational practice. It is interesting to note that while Lisa experienced administrative support and recognition for her work, Guadalupe experienced less administrative support and was reprimanded for voicing her concerns about the reading program. Lisa's position as a tenured, middle-class, Euro-American woman and Guadalupe's position as an emergency-credentialed, working-class Latina woman might be factors contributing to the amount of administrative support they received and the amount of stress they experienced due to their tenured and nontenured status and their work with students who faced formidable barriers. Segura-Mora (1998) and Castillo (1998) discuss the choices they made as critical bicultural educators of color when confronted with similar obstacles. When they reached a point where they no longer felt effective, they channeled their efforts into other areas of educational need, but they did not abandon their critical stance.

FIGURE **3** ■

- Mandated scripted curriculum and instructional programs
- Lack of administrative support
- Isolation and lack of support from colleagues
- Physical burnout if too many commitments to school, classroom, and community activities
- Emotional burnout if not able to work in mutually supportive relationships with other critical educators and community representatives
- Lack of mentors who practice critical pedagogy
- Few opportunities to share findings from classroom experiences in journals, presentations, or teacher circles (because of a lack of a forum for critical educators and time limitations)
- Limited access to other critical educators
- Stress from need to work with school, district, and state educational policies and practices that are inconsistent with liberatory educational values

Obstacles to Critical Pedagogy

Critical educators, like all teachers, desire affirmation from colleagues, family, and friends. They attempt to work in community with other teachers in order to share stories, learn from one another, and receive and give sustenance so that they may continue to move forward. Time for respite and reflection, whether found in spiritual sanctuary or within circles of family and friends, is essential for one's mental, physical, emotional, and spiritual balance. Teaching is challenging work, and when one is working within a system that is diametrically opposed to one's beliefs, ideas, and vision of possibilities, the challenge can become oppressive. Figure 4 lists ways that critical educators can relieve some

FIGURE **4** ■

> - Develop supportive relationships with like-minded colleagues.
> - Create "culture circles" or teacher circles to share ideas, critique, and support each other.
> - Take care of physical, mental, and spiritual needs.
> - Take time to reflect.
> - Focus locally and then globally.
> - Realize that what they do is important and vital though not always appreciated or recognized.
> - Continue to grow personally and professionally.
> - Diversify experiences with different educational settings as needed.
> - Enlist the support of community resource people and parents, and connect with others working for radical change inside and outside of the educational field (e.g., in social work, labor, and community organizing).
> - Experience joy in their work.

Ways Critical Teachers Can Stay Effective ■

of the stress they experience. Critical educators such as Guadalupe and Lisa, who are struggling to change educational policy and practices through reflection and action, must find ways to refresh themselves, transform their practice, and renew their joy in the act of teaching.

Conclusion

Educating English Language Learners With Special Education Needs: Trends and Future Directions

Leonard M. Baca, *University of Colorado at Boulder*

Since the 1970s, when our field first began paying attention to the needs of English language learners with disabilities, educators have repeatedly raised two questions: Are we identifying the right students, and are we providing appropriate instruction for these students?

Initially, special educators working with English language learners advocated bilingual approaches to assessment and instruction, but they soon concluded that adapting existing practices and services was unlikely to improve the educational attainment of these learners. In the special education field as a whole, there was little consensus on fundamental issues. Educators did not agree on definitions of disabilities, and they were increasingly concerned about the questionable criteria used to identify students for special education, the absence of special teaching methods for students with disabilities, and the ineffectiveness of special education programs (Chaflant, 1989).

In recent years, a growing number of special educators working with English language learners have questioned many of the basic assumptions behind special education practice (Bogdan & Kugelmass, 1984):

- **Disability is a condition that individuals have.**
  To assume that disabilities reside in individuals is to ignore the impact of the environment on student performance.

- **The terms *disabled* and *typical* are useful and objective distinctions.**
  The use of labels such as *disabled* and *typical* does not promote inclusive philosophies and practices.

- **Special education is a coordinated and rationally conceived system of services that helps children identified as disabled.**
  Services for English language learners with disabilities are not always well conceived. Students are not always taught with adequate first language and English as a second language (ESL) support, and special education services are often poorly coordinated.

- **Progress in special education is made through improvements in diagnosis, intervention, and technology.**
  Schools cannot provide effective special education services for English language learners by simply adapting services that have been designed for English speakers and that do not take into account the linguistic, cultural, and other background characteristics of English language learners.

According to Rueda (1989), educators can respond to the present system of special education services for English language learners in three ways: They can maintain, improve, or restructure the system. Those who maintain the system focus on improving compliance with its regulated practices; those who wish to improve the system attempt to refine those practices; and those who want to restructure the system question its underlying assumptions and seek to fundamentally change practices to address broader social and educational issues. Restructuring might involve, for example, doing away with standardized tests in favor of a more student-centered approach that looks at a particular child's performance in a particular class with a particular teacher. In place of the present practice of deferring assistance to students until they meet special education eligibility criteria, students might receive services as soon as they are needed, and bilingual education, English as a second language, general education, and special education programs would be integrated. These are the kinds of reform advocated by Baca and de Valenzuela (1994) and Rueda (1989, 1990).

The trends that the authors in this book describe and the recommendations that they make are designed both to improve and restructure the special education system. The recommendations address three broad areas: prevention and early intervention, assessment, and instruction. This chapter summarizes the best practices recommended by the authors in these three areas and concludes with a brief discussion of future directions.

Prevention and Early Intervention

Through prevention of school failure and early intervention strategies for students experiencing academic difficulties, the general education system can enhance students' academic success and reduce inappropriate special education referrals. If English language learners with special needs are to be included in general education classes, a variety of reforms are needed. In particular, schools need to provide students with optimal learning environments and instruction that views the students' native languages and cultures as rich resources on which to build.

Ortiz (this volume) makes an important distinction between students who have disabilities and students who do not have disabilities but fall behind because the school has not met their needs. Early intervention strategies are necessary to distinguish between these students. Such strategies increase the likelihood of academic success for both those who need additional support within the general education system and those who need special education services. For students with disabilities, the documentation of early intervention efforts helps school staff understand which interventions worked and which did not as they design individualized education plans.

The practice of early intervention for failing students is not a new one (Graden, Casey, & Christenson, 1985; Maheady, Towne, Algozzine, Mercer, & Ysseldyke, 1983). Baca, de Valenzuela, and García (1996) have developed a prevention and enhancement programming (PEP) model. The PEP model includes many of the components described by Ortiz (this volume) as well as other factors crucial to the success of English language learners.

The major components of the PEP model are coordination among programs, consistency of services from year to year, and collaboration among staff members and between staff and family and community members. Different school programs (such as Title I, English as a second language, bilingual, general education, and special education) are often uncoordinated (Skrtic, 1988), and their curricula must be aligned. School staff can foster a collegial spirit of collaboration by emphasizing joint responsibility for all students, providing joint instructional planning time, and enlisting the support of administrators for school improvement initiatives that focus on English language learners. Including family members as equal partners in educational planning, instruction, and student and program evaluation is an important part of collaborative efforts.

Assessment

Improving practices and procedures for assessing English language learners who are referred to special education has been a tremendous challenge for school psychologists, assessment personnel, speech pathologists, and special educators. Although new models of assessment have been developed and improved instruments and procedures are available, little progress has been made in eliminating bias in the assessment of English language learners. Meaningful reform for these students requires changes in existing paradigms, practices, and procedures.

Toward a New Assessment Paradigm

Figueroa (this volume) recommends eliminating current methods used to assess students suspected of having learning disabilities, mild retardation, or communication disorders. Instead, careful observation of students in an optimal learning environment, over an extended period of time, allows teachers to document students' strengths and weaknesses and provide the necessary data to make clinical judgments about the presence of disabilities. Such observations are more valid than test scores to determine special education eligibility. As suggested by Figueroa, changes in special education legislation, or waivers of existing mandates, will be needed if federal special education funds are to be used to design optimal learning environments. While lobbying aggressively for this flexibility is important, changing federal laws will take time. In the meantime, assessment personnel will continue to rely on existing practices, making it important to minimize biases inherent in traditional processes.

Most current assessment practices are based on the medical and psychometric model, which assumes that a diagnosed disability is an objective, knowable reality and that society is culturally and linguistically homogeneous. Given current thinking about disabilities as socially constructed phenomena that cannot be located solely within individuals, and given the reality of our diverse, heterogeneous society, these assumptions are clearly no longer tenable. Mercer (1992) critiques the psychometric and medical model, contrasting it with the interpretive, social system model:

> Where the psychomedical model sees "mental retardation" as an objective empirical fact, the social system model sees it as a social construction. Because the definition of "mental

retardation" is socially negotiated, it not only varies from society to society but changes over time. Where the psychomedical model sees "mental retardation" as a disability that one . "has," the interpretive model sees it as a status that one holds as a result of a variety of social contingencies. A person can be "retarded" in one group and not in another. Retardation is a social enactment. (p. 25)

An interpretive, social system model views the student within social contexts and evaluates the effects of these influences on student performance. In contrast to a psychometric model that relies on standardized, norm-referenced tests, the interpretive model uses criterion-referenced tests and informal assessment strategies. Multiple measures and techniques are used in student assessments, including, for example, curriculum-based tests, interviews, rating scales, portfolios, and teacher observations. Academic performance is considered within the larger contexts of the school, classroom, playground, peer group, family, and community. Other factors that contribute to the student's apparent difficulties are identified. Assessments are conducted in both the native language and in English, as appropriate, and acculturation and learning styles are examined. That the problem lies within the student is the very last possibility considered, after all other factors that might explain the problems are eliminated.

Ortiz and Yates (this volume) present a framework for planning and conducting assessments of English language learners. Their framework takes into account special factors (e.g., prior instruction or language proficiency) that may influence, or explain, student performance. Because eligibility decisions are based largely on interpretations of assessment outcomes, assessors must have expertise in the evaluation of English language learners. Assessors must conduct assessments in the student's native language, as well as in English, to provide a comprehensive view of what the student knows and can do, regardless of the language in which knowledge and skills are demonstrated. Assessment instruments used must be valid and reliable. In the absence of such instruments, assessors must determine appropriate adaptations, being sure to fully disclose in their evaluation reports the limitations of results from nonstandard administrations. Results of norm-referenced testing should be supported by results of informal curriculum-based measures of student performance. The multidisciplinary team—the group of education professionals responsible for determining eligibility for special education services—must be confident that learning problems are not the result of a disability and not the result of other factors such as lack of academic support, limited English proficiency, and cultural differences.

Other practical suggestions for using this approach to assessment to determine language skills, level of acculturation, cognitive development, learning styles, and cultural orientation can be found on a CD-ROM on assessment developed by the Bueno Center for Multicultural Education (2001a).

Parent Involvement in Assessment

García (this volume) makes a strong case for the meaningful involvement of parents in the assessment of their children. School staff need to involve parents not only to comply with legislative requirements but also to obtain a complete and accurate picture of students' strengths and weaknesses in nonacademic environments such as the home and community. Because cultural values play a strong role in shaping parents' roles and comfort level in the assessment process, school personnel need to be knowledgeable about the family's cultural background if the school and family are to forge a productive partnership. Shifting from a psychometric assessment model to a social system model increases the importance of parental participation in the assessment process. A CD-ROM on parent involvement by the Bueno Center for Multicultural Education (2001b) is a valuable resource for facilitating parental involvement in the special education assessment process.

Instruction

Culturally Responsive Instructional Planning

Cloud (this volume) outlines an instructional planning process that ensures effective instruction for English language learners with special education needs. Because effective instruction is culturally responsive, creating a culturally responsive teaching and learning environment is central to the instructional planning process. In a culturally responsive class, the teacher strives to ensure that all elements of the learning and teaching environment—curricula and materials, instructional strategies, classroom interactions, classroom resources, counseling, and parent outreach efforts—are as culturally compatible as possible with student preferences and background experiences.

Cloud addresses a commonly asked question: Should literacy be taught in the native language for English language learners with disabilities? It is a common belief in the field that for students with disabilities who are experiencing difficulty learning to read and write in their first language, literacy instruction should be in English because the disability interferes with native language instruction. Cloud dispels this myth, citing research showing that all students, whatever their ability level, benefit from native language instruction. This does not mean that English language development should be ignored. Rather, it argues for introducing English when the student is developmentally ready to benefit from instruction in it.

Cloud stresses that instruction for English language learners with special education needs should meet the same high standards as instruction provided other children. To ensure that learners with special education needs are held to the highest possible academic standards, teachers should develop individualized education program (IEP) goals and objectives in relation to state and national curriculum standards, including ESL standards. To achieve these high standards, English language learners with disabilities require "double sheltering"—that is, instruction that both provides comprehensible language input and accommodates learning disabilities (e.g., by providing instruction consistent with students' preferred learning styles and attention span).

The final component of the instructional planning process is a culturally and linguistically responsive family service plan. This plan requires that staff obtain information about the family's level of acculturation, cultural beliefs regarding the disability, familiarity with the school system and procedures, and preferred communication styles. In short, the instructional planning process must take into account student differences in culture, language, and disability. School staff must consider each of these differences individually without losing sight of the end goal—an integrated instructional plan.

Effective Instruction

Much has been written in recent years about the value of providing scaffolding within Vygotsky's (1978) notion of the zone of proximal development (ZPD). However, little has been written on how to use these scaffolds with English language learners with disabilities. Santamaría, Fletcher, and Bos (this volume) describe how three kinds of scaffolding strategies—mediated, task, and materials—promote learning. To these three strategies, they add a fourth, Krashen's (1982b) concept of comprehensible input. Comprehensible input is a scaffolding technique in that the language of instruction is within students' zone of proximal development. When the language of instruction is presented clearly, with meaningful examples and familiar props, comprehension is enhanced.

Drawing from the research of Tharp, Estrada, Dalton, and Yamauchi (2000) and Jiménez and Gersten (1999), Santamaría and her colleagues present five pedagogical principles that are known to be effective with English language learners of all ability levels:

- Work collaboratively with students.
- Develop language and literacy across the curriculum.
- Connect school to students' lives.
- Teach complex thinking.
- Teach through conversation.

In classes that reflect these principles, students work collaboratively in small groups, creating a community of learners. Whether the setting is ESL, special education, or general education, students are provided a rich array of language learning opportunities. Developing language is a responsibility of not only the language arts teachers but of all teachers.

Learning is enhanced when teachers connect what students already know to what they need to know. Luis Moll (1992) calls on educators to use the vast "funds of knowledge" that exist within the home culture as the basis for learning activities. English language learners with learning disabilities are much more likely to succeed academically when the school reaches out to them in an effort to make schoolwork compatible with their daily lives.

The standards movement, which emphasizes the importance of holding all students, regardless of language background, to the same high academic standards, has particular importance for English language learners with disabilities. In the past, instruction for these students has tended to be remedial and reductionist rather than complex and challenging. Yet when these students are challenged to engage in higher order complex thinking, they rise to the occasion (Ortiz & Wilkinson, 1991).

In recent years, much has been written about the importance of fostering instructional conversations. Yet because of the prevalence of large-group instruction in our schools, opportunities for extended conversations in class are very limited. What is needed is a reconfiguration of classroom design and student grouping. Such a reconfiguration allows the teacher to engage small groups of students in meaningful and extended conversations, with the teacher becoming a facilitator of small-group instruction. English language learners with disabilities thrive with the added individual attention they receive during small-group conversations (Fillmore & Valadez, 1986; Willig, Swedo, & Ortiz, 1987).

Barbara Goldstein (this volume) stresses the importance of critical pedagogy for English language learners with disabilities. As Goldstein

(1996b) has written elsewhere, in critical pedagogy, the "teacher creates the conditions in the classroom for students to become empowered by becoming aware of the presence of knowledge and power in their own lives that oppress and liberate" (p. 32). According to Goldstein, it has not been difficult to integrate the best practices in special education for English language learners with critical pedagogy, as there is a good fit between what these student need and what critical pedagogy can provide.

Future Directions

As an emerging field, special education for English language learners continues to evolve as the number of students from culturally diverse backgrounds increases. The changing demography and the unique backgrounds and needs of these students challenge us to improve our theoretical perspectives and professional practices. We have seen that many of the standard assumptions in the field of special education do not apply to English language learners. For example, if we question the assumption that a disability is a measurable and disabling condition and replace it with the assumption that all students, whatever their level of ability, can learn, then what use do we have for traditional special education diagnostic classifications? When students are referred to special education, doesn't it make sense to place them in a regular classroom with a teacher who can document their strengths and weaknesses as a way to determine if, in fact, they have disabilities that require special education services?

With the change from the old behaviorist model of disability to a sociocultural framework, special educators working with English language learners must adopt a new set of assumptions and practices. We recommend the following as guiding principles for the future:

- All children, including English language learners with disabilities, can learn.
- Early intervention strategies can prevent academic failure.
- The native languages and cultures of students are strengths on which to build.

- Students who are not succeeding in school need a challenging, not a remedial, curriculum.
- English language learners with disabilities should be educated in inclusive environments.

These new assumptions have implications for the roles that special education teachers will play in the future. The need for a variety of program services, along with an emphasis on inclusive education, means that the special education teacher of the future will not function independently in an isolated, self-contained class or resource room. Rather, that teacher will work as a consultant to and a collaborator with colleagues in general education classes. This new role for special educators will require changes in teacher preparation and ongoing professional development. The separation of regular and special education into distinct and independent programs will give way to a more unified school organization with the goal of serving all students in an inclusive environment. All of our students deserve the best education we can give them. We should not settle for less.

References

Abedi, J. (1999a). *Differences between response patterns of LEP and non-LEP to standardized test items.* Los Angeles: University of California, National Center for Research on Evaluation, Standards, and Student Testing (CRESST).

Abedi, J. (1999b, April). *The impact of students' background characteristics on accommodation results for students with limited English proficiency.* Paper presented at the meeting of the American Educational Research Association, Montreal, Canada.

Abedi, J. (1999c, April). *NAEP math test accommodations for students with limited English proficiency.* Paper presented at the meeting of the American Educational Research Association, Montreal, Canada.

Abedi, J. (2000, April). *Confounding students' performance and their language background.* Paper presented at the meeting of the American Educational Research Association, New Orleans, LA.

Abedi, J., Hoffstetter, C., Baker, E. L., & Lord, C. (1998). *NAEP math performance and test accommodations: Interactions with students' language background* (CSE Technical Report). Los Angeles: University of California, Center for the Study of Evaluation.

Abedi, J., Lord, C., & Hoffstetter, C. (1998). *Impact of selected background variables on students' NAEP math performance.* Los Angeles: University of California, National Center for Research on Evaluation, Standards, and Student Testing (CRESST).

Abedi, J., Lord, C., & Plummer, J. (1995). *Language background as a variable in NAEP mathematics performance. NAEP TRP Task 3D: Language background study.* Los Angeles: University of California, Center for the Study of Evaluation (CSE).

Adelman, H. (1970). An interactive view of causality. *Academic Therapy, 6,* 43-52.

American Educational Research Association. (1985). *Standards for educational and psychological testing.* Washington, DC: American Psychological Association and National Council on Measurement in Education.

American Educational Research Association. (1999). *Standards for educational and psychological testing.* Washington, DC: American Psychological Association and National Council on Measurement in Education.

Anderson, L. W., & Pellicer, L. O. (1998). Toward an understanding of unusually successful programs for economically disadvantaged students. *Journal of Education for Students Placed at Risk, 3*(3), 237-263.

Anderson, N. E., & Olson, J. (1996, August). *Puerto Rico assessment of educational progress: 1996 PRAEP technical report.* Princeton, NJ: Educational Testing Service.

Artiles, A. J. (2000, July). *The inclusive education movement and minority representation in special education: Trends, paradoxes, and dilemmas.* Keynote address delivered at the International Special Education Conference, Manchester, England.

Artiles, A. J., Rueda, R., Salazar, I., & Higareda, I. (2000, November). *Factors associated with English learner representation in special education: Emerging evidence from urban school districts in California.* Paper presented at the conference on Minority Issues in Special Education in the Public Schools, Harvard University, Cambridge, MA.

Artiles, A. J., & Trent, S. C. (1994). Overrepresentation of minority students in special education: A continuing debate. *Journal of Special Education, 27*, 410-437.

Artiles, A. J., & Trent, S. C. (2000). Representation of culturally/linguistically diverse students. In C. R. Reynolds & E. Fletcher-Jantzen (Eds.), *Encyclopedia of special education: Vol. 1* (2nd ed., pp. 513-517). New York: John Wiley & Sons.

Artiles, A. J., Trent, S. C., Hoffman-Kipp, P., & López-Torres, L. (2000). From individual acquisition to cultural-historical practices in multicultural teacher education. *Remedial and Special Education, 21*, 79-91.

Artiles, A. J., Trent, S. C., & Palmer, J. (in press). Culturally diverse students in special education: Legacies and prospects. In J. A. Banks & C. M. Banks (Eds.), *Handbook of research on multicultural education* (2nd ed.). San Francisco: Jossey Bass.

Artiles, A. J., & Zamora-Durán, G. (Eds.). (1997). *Reducing disproportionate representation of culturally diverse students in special and gifted education.* Reston, VA: Council for Exceptional Children.

Au, K. H., & Jordan, C. (1981). Teaching reading to Hawaiian children: Finding culturally appropriate solutions. In H. Trueba, G. P. Guthrie, and K. H. Au (Eds.), *Culture in the bilingual classroom: Studies in classroom ethnography* (pp. 139-152). Rowley, MA: Newbury House.

August, D., & Hakuta, K. (Eds.). (1997). *Improving schooling for language minority children: A research agenda.* Washington, DC: National Academy Press.

Baca, L. (1990). Theory and practice in bilingual/cross-cultural special education: Major issues and implications for research, practice, and policy. In *Proceedings of the First Research Symposium on Limited English Proficient Student Issues* (pp. 247-280). Washington, DC: Office of Bilingual Education and Minority Languages Affairs.

Baca, L. (1998). Bilingual special education: A judicial perspective. In L. Baca & H. Cervantes (Eds.), *The bilingual special education interface* (pp. 76-97). Upper Saddle River, NJ: Prentice Hall.

Baca, L., & Cervantes, H. (1984). *The bilingual special education interface.* St. Louis, MO: Times Mirror/Mosby.

Baca, L., & de Valenzuela, J. S. (1994). *Reconstructing the bilingual special education interface* (Program Information Guide, No. 20). Washington, DC: National Clearinghouse for Bilingual Education. Retrieved May 20, 2002, from http://www.ncbe.gwu.edu/ncbepubs/pigs/pig20.htm

Baca, L., & de Valenzuela, J. S. (1998). Background and rationale for bilingual special education. In L. Baca & H. Cervantes (Eds.), *The bilingual special education interface* (pp. 2-25). Upper Saddle River, NJ: Prentice Hall.

Baca, L., de Valenzuela, J. S., & García, S. B. (1996). *A new approach to prereferral intervention: The PEP model.* Boulder: University of Colorado at Boulder, BUENO Center for Multicultural Education.

Bachus, A., & O'Connell, M. (1998). *Fertility of American women: Current population reports.* Washington, DC: U.S. Census Bureau.

Bailey, D. B., Jr., Skinner, D., Rodriguez, P., Gut, K., & Correa, V. (1999). Awareness, use and satisfaction with services for Latino parents of young children with disabilities. *Exceptional Children, 65,* 367-381.

Barr, M. (1997, February/March). Linking learning and assessment. *Thrust for Educational Leadership,* 4-7.

Bilingual Education Act, Title VII of the Elementary and Secondary Act of 1968. Pub. L. No. 90-247, 20 U.S.C. § 880b-1.

Bogdan, R., & Kugelmass, J. (1984). Case studies of mainstreaming: A symbolic interactionist approach to special schooling. In L. Barton & S. Tomlinson (Eds.), *Special education and social interests* (pp. 173-191). New York: Nichols.

Boone, R. S., Wolfe, P. S., & Schaufler, J. H. (1999). Written communication in special education: Meeting the needs of culturally and linguistically diverse families. *Multiple Voices for Ethnically Diverse Exceptional Learners, 3*(1), 25-36.

Brislin, R. (1993). *Understanding culture's influence on behavior.* Fort Worth, TX: Harcourt Brace.

Brophy, J. (1992). Probing the subtleties of subject-matter teaching. *Educational Leadership, 49*(7), 4-8.

Bruck, M. (1982). Language disabled children: Performance in an additive bilingual education program. *Applied Psycholinguistics, 3,* 45-60.

Bueno Center for Multicultural Education. (2001a). *Assessment* [CD-ROM]. University of Colorado Boulder: Author. (Available from BUENO Center for Multicultural Education, University of Colorado Boulder, Campus Box 249, Boulder, CO 80309; tel: 303-492-5416; e-mail: BUENOCTR@colorado.edu)

Bueno Center for Multicultural Education. (2001b). *Parent involvement* [CD-ROM]. University of Colorado at Boulder: Author. (Available from BUENO Center for Multicultural Education, University of Colorado Boulder, Campus Box 249, Boulder, CO 80309; tel: 303-492-5416; e-mail: BUENOCTR@colorado.edu)

Burke, M. D., Hagan, S. L., & Grossen, B. (1998). What curricular design and strategies accommodate diverse learners? *Teaching Exceptional Children, 31*(1), 34-38.

Carreira, M., & Armengol, R. (2001). Professional opportunities for heritage language speakers. In J. K. Peyton, D. A. Ranard, & S. McGinnis (Eds.), *Heritage languages in America: Preserving a national resource* (pp.109-136). McHenry, IL and Washington, DC: Delta Sytems and Center for Applied Linguistics.

Cartledge, G., & Milburn, J. F. (Eds.). (1996). *Cultural diversity and social skills instruction.* Champaign, IL: Research Press.

Castillo, G. M. (1998). Education as the practice of freedom. In J. Frederickson (Series Ed.) and A. Darder (Vol. Ed.), *Reclaiming our voices: Emancipatory narratives on critical literacy, praxis, and pedagogy. Teaching as an act of love: Reflections on Paulo Freire and his contributions to our lives and our work* (pp. 43-46). Los Angeles: California Association for Bilingual Education.

Cavanaugh, M. (1999). *An implementation guide for Neverstreaming.* Elk Grove, CA: Elk Grove Unified School District.

Chacon, V. (1999). *Batería Woodcock-Muñoz prueba de aprovechamiento revisada.* Unpublished manuscript, University of Arizona, Tucson.

Chalfant, J. C. (1989). Learning disabilities: Policy issues and promising approaches. *American Psychologist, 44,* 392-398.

Chalfant, J. C., & Pysh, M. V. D. (1989). Teacher Assistance Teams: Five descriptive studies on 96 teams. *Remedial and Special Education, 10*(6), 49-58.

Chalfant, J. C., Pysh, M. V. D., & Moultrie, R. (1979). Teacher Assistance Teams: A model for within-building problem solving. *Learning Disability Quarterly, 2*(3), 85-96.

Chamot, A. U., & O'Malley, J. M. (1994). *The CALLA handbook: Implementing the Cognitive Academic Language Learning Approach.* Reading, MA: Addison-Wesley.

Chamot, A. U., & O'Malley, M. (1996). Implementing the cognitive academic language learning approach (CALLA). In R. Oxford (Ed.), *Language learning strategies around the world: Cross-cultural perspectives* (pp. 167-173). Honolulu: University of Hawai'i, Second Language Teaching and Curriculum Center.

Cheng, L. L. (1997). Diversity: Challenges and implications for assessment. *Journal of Children's Communication Development, 19*(1), 55-62.

Civil Rights Act of 1964, Pub. L. No. 88-352, 42 U.S.C. § 2000 *et seq.*

Clay, M. (1985). *The early detection of reading difficulties.* Portsmouth, NH: Heinemann.

Cloud, N. (1990). Planning and implementing an English as a second language program. In A. Carrasquillo & R. E. Baecher (Eds.), *Teaching the bilingual special education student* (pp. 106-131). Norwood, NJ: Ablex.

Cloud, N. (1993). Language, culture and disability: Implications for instruction and teacher preparation. *Teacher Education and Special Education, 16*(1), 60-72.

Cloud, N. (1994). Special education needs of second language students. In F. Genesee (Ed.), *Educating second language children: The whole child, the whole curriculum, the whole community* (pp. 243-277). New York: Cambridge University Press.

Cloud, N., Genesee, F., & Hamayan, E. (2000). *Dual language instruction: A handbook for enriched education.* Boston: Heinle & Heinle.

Coles, G. (1987). *The learning mystique: A critical look at "learning disabilities."* New York: Pantheon.

Collier, V. P. (1995a). *Acquiring a second language for school* (Directions in Language and Education, Vol. 1, No. 4). Washington, DC: National Clearinghouse for Bilingual Education. Retrieved October 23, 2001, from http://www.ncbe.gwu.edu/ncbepubs/directions/04.htm

Collier, V. P. (1995b). *Promoting academic success for ESL students: Understanding second language acquisition for school.* Elizabeth, NJ: New Jersey Teachers of English to Speakers of Other Languages–Bilingual Educators.

Cooper, K. L., & Rascon, L. (1994). *Building positive relationships on the border with parents of special students: Effective practices for the I.E.P.* (ERIC Document Reproduction Service No. ED 369 627)

Cummins, J. (1981). Four misconceptions about language proficiency in bilingual education. *National Association for Bilingual Education Journal, 5*(3), 31-45.

Cummins, J. (1984). *Bilingualism and special education: Issues in assessment and pedagogy.* Clevedon, Avon, UK: Multilingual Matters.

Cummins, J. (1986). Empowering language minority students. *Harvard Educational Review, 56,* 18-36.

Cummins, J. (1989). A theoretical framework for bilingual special education. *Exceptional Children, 56*(2), 111-119.

Cummins, J. (1994a). From coercive to collaborative relations of power in the teaching of literacy. In B. M. Ferdman, R. Weber, & A. Ramirez (Eds.), *Literacy across languages and cultures* (pp. 295-331). Albany: State University of New York Press.

Cummins, J. (1994b). Knowledge, power, and identity in teaching English as a second language. In F. Genesee (Ed.), *Educating second language children: The whole child, the whole curriculum, the whole community* (pp. 103-125). Cambridge, UK: Cambridge University Press.

Dalton, E. (1989). *IDEA Oral Language Proficiency Test.* Whittier, CA: Ballard & Tighe.

Damico, J. S. (1991). Descriptive assessment of communicative ability in limited English proficient students. In E. V. Hamayan & J. S. Damico (Eds.), *Limiting bias in the assessment of bilingual students* (pp. 157-217). Austin, TX: Pro-Ed.

Darder, A. (1991). *Culture and power in the classroom.* New York: Bergin & Garvey.

Darsie, M. L. (1926). The mental capacity of American-born Japanese children. *Comparative Psychology Monographs, 3,* 1-89.

de Valenzuela, J. S., Connery, M. C., & Musanti, S. (2000). The theoretical foundations of professional development in special education: Is sociocultural theory enough? *Remedial and Special Education, 21*(2), 111-120.

Diana v. State Board of Education, No. C-70-37 (N. D. CA 1970).

Diaz-Greenberg, R. (1997). The emergence of voice in Latino students: A critical approach. In J. Frederickson (Ed.), *Reclaiming our voices: Emancipatory narratives on critical literacy, praxis, and pedagogy. An occasional paper series for entering the 21st century* (pp. 24-38). Los Angeles: California Association for Bilingual Education.

Donovan, S. & Cross, C. (Eds.). (2002). *Minority students in special and gifted education.* Washington, DC: National Academy Press.

Dornic, S. (1977). *Information processing and bilingualism.* Stockholm: University of Stockholm, Department of Psychology.

Dornic, S. (1978). *Noise and language dominance.* Stockholm: University of Stockholm, Department of Psychology.

Dornic, S. (1979). Information processing in bilinguals: Some selected issues. *Psychological Research, 40,* 329-348.

Duncan, S. E., & De Avila, E. A. (1990). *Language Assessment Scales–Oral (LAS-O)*. Monterey, CA: CTB/McGraw-Hill.

Dunn, L. L. (1968). Special education for the mildly retarded: Is much of it justified? *Exceptional Children, 35*, 5-22.

Durán, R. P. (1983). *Hispanics' education and background.* New York: College Entrance Examination Board.

Dyrcia S. et al. v. Board of Education of the City of New York, 79 c. 2562 (E.D.N.Y. 1979).

Dyson, A. (1999). Inclusion and inclusions: Theories and discourses in inclusive education. In H. Daniels & P. Garner (Eds.), *World yearbook of education 1999: Inclusive education* (pp. 36-53). London: Kogan Page.

Echevarría, J. (1995). An alternative reading approach: Instructional conversations in a bilingual special education setting. *Learning Disabilities Research and Practice, 10*(2), 108-119.

Echevarría, J., & Graves, A. (1998). *Sheltered content instruction. Teaching English language learners with diverse abilities.* Boston: Allyn & Bacon.

Echevarría, J., Vogt, M. E., & Short, D. J. (2000). *Making content comprehensible for English language learners: The SIOP model.* Boston: Allyn & Bacon.

Education for all Handicapped Children Act of 1975, Pub. L. No. 94-142, § 1400 et seq.

Elmore, R. F., & Fuhrman, S. H. (1994). Governing curriculum: Changing patterns in policy, politics, and practice. In R. F. Elmore & S. H. Fuhrman (Eds.), *The governance of curriculum: 1994 Yearbook of the Association for Supervision and Curriculum Development* (pp. 1-10). Alexandria, VA: ASCD.

Englert, C. S., & Marriage, T. (1996). A sociocultural perspective: Teaching ways-of-thinking and ways-of-talking in a literacy community. *Learning Disabilities Research and Practice, 11*, 157-167.

Enguidanos, T., & Ruiz, N. T. (1997). Traigan sus vidas, yo traigo la mía: Shared reading for older, emergent readers in bilingual classrooms. In L. Denti & P. T. Cousins (Eds.), *New ways of looking at learning disabilities* (pp. 199-222). Denver, CO: Love.

Erikson, F., & Mohatt, G. (1982). The cultural organization of participation structure in two classrooms of Indian students. In G. Spindler (Ed.), *Doing the ethnography of schooling* (pp. 132-174). New York: Holt, Rhinehart, & Winston.

Farr, B. P., & Trumbull, E. (1997). *Assessment alternatives for diverse classrooms.* Norwood, MA: Christopher-Gordon.

Fashola, O. S., & Slavin, R. E. (1998). Schoolwide reform models. What works? *Phi Delta Kappan, 79*, 370-379.

Fern, V., Anstrom, K., & Silcox, B. (1994). *Active learning and the limited English proficient student* (Directions in Language and Education, Vol. 1, No. 2). Washington, DC: National Clearinghouse for Bilingual Education. Retrieved October 23, 2001, from http://www.ncbe.gwu.edu/ncbepubs/directions/02.htm

Feuerstein, R. (1979). *The dynamic assessment of retarded performers: The learning potential assessment device. Theory, instruments, and techniques.* Baltimore: University Park Press.

Figueroa, R. A. (1990). Best practices in the assessment of bilingual children. In A. Thomas & J. Grimes (Eds.), *Best practices in school psychology II* (pp. 93-106). Washington, DC: National Association of School Psychologists.

Figueroa, R. A. (2000). T*he role of limited English proficiency in special education identification and intervention.* Washington, DC: National Research Council.

Figueroa, R. A., & García, E. (1994). Issues in testing students from culturally and linguistically diverse backgrounds. *Multicultural Education, 2,* 10-23.

Figueroa, R. A., & Hernandez, S. (2000). *Our nation on the fault line: Hispanic American education. Testing Hispanic students in the United States: Technical and policy issues.* Washington, DC: President's Advisory Commission on Educational Excellence for Hispanic Americans.

Fillmore, L. W. (1991). Language and cultural issues in early education. In S. L. Kagan (Ed.), *The care and education of America's young children: Obstacles and opportunities. Nineteenth yearbook of the National Society for the Study of Education* (pp. 30-49). Chicago: National Society for the Study of Education.

Fillmore, L. W., & Valadez, C. (1986). Teaching bilingual learners. In M. C. Wittrock (Ed.), *Handbook of research on teaching* (pp. 648-685). New York: Macmillan.

Finn, J. D. (1982). Patterns in special education placement as revealed by the OCR surveys. In K. A. Heller, W. H. Holtzman, & S. Messick (Eds.), *Placing children in special education: A strategy for equity* (pp. 322-381). Washington, DC: National Academy Press.

Flores, B., Rueda, R., & Porter, B. (1986). Examining assumptions and instructional practices related to the acquisition of literacy with bilingual special education students. In A. C. Willig & H. F. Greenburg (Eds.), *Bilingualism and learning disabilities* (pp. 149-165). New York: American Library.

Ford, B. A. (1995). African American community involvement processes and special education: Essential networks for effective education. In B. A. Ford, F. E. Obiakor, & J. M. Patton (Eds.), *Effective education for African American exceptional learners* (pp. 235-272). Austin, TX: Pro-Ed.

Frank, R. A. (1993). *Critical cartography: Mapping teachers' journeys toward critical pedagogy.* Unpublished doctoral dissertation, Claremont Graduate School, Claremont, CA.

Freeman, D. E., & Freeman, Y. S. (1993). Strategies for promoting the primary languages of all students. *The Reading Teacher, 46*(7), 552-558.

Freire, P. (1970). *Pedagogy of the oppressed.* New York: Seabury.

Freire, P. (1973). *Education for critical consciousness.* New York: Continuum.

Freire, P. (1985). *The politics of education.* New York: Bergin & Garvey.

Freire, P., & Macedo, D. (1987). *Literacy: Reading the word and the world.* Boston: Bergin & Garvey.

Fromkin, V., & Rodman, R. (1988). *An introduction to language* (4th ed.). New York: Holt, Rinehart, & Winston.

Frymier, J., & Gansnedner, B. (1989). The Phi Delta Kappan study of students at risk. *Phi Delta Kappan, 71*, 142-146.

Fuchs, D., Fuchs, L. S., Bahr, M. W., Fernstrom, P., & Stecker, P. M. (1990). Pre-referral intervention: A prescriptive approach. *Exceptional Children, 56*, 493-513.

Gallimore, R., & Goldberg, C. (2001). Analyzing cultural models and settings to connect minority achievement and school improvement research. *Educational Psychologist, 36*(1), 45-56.

Gándara, P. (1999). *Second language acquisition and academic achievement.* San Francisco: WestEd.

García, E. (1992). Teachers for language minority students: Evaluating professional standards. In *Proceedings of the second national research symposium on limited English proficient students' issues: Focus on evaluation and measurement, Vol. 1* (pp. 383-414). Washington, DC: U.S. Department of Education, Office of Bilingual Education and Minority Languages Affairs.

García, S. B., & Dominguez, L. (1997). Cultural contexts that influence learning and academic performance. In L. B. Silver (Ed.), *Child and adolescent psychiatric clinics of North America: Academic difficulties* (pp. 621-655). Philadelphia: W. B. Saunders.

García, S. B., & Malkin, D. H. (1993). Toward defining programs and services for culturally and linguistically diverse learners in special education. *Teaching Exceptional Children, 26*(1), 52-58.

Garcia, S. B., Méndez Pérez, A., & Ortiz, A. A. (2000). Interpreting Mexican American mothers' beliefs about language disabilities from a sociocultural perspective: Implications for early childhood intervention. *Remedial and Special Education, 21*(2), 90-100.

García, S. B., & Ortiz, A. A. (1988). *Preventing inappropriate referrals of language minority students to special education* (New Focus, No.5). Wheaton, MD: National Clearinghouse for Bilingual Education. Retrieved May 20, 2002, from
http://www.ncbe.gwu.edu/ ncbepubs/classics/focus/05referral.htm

García, S. B., Wilkinson, C. Y., & Ortiz, A. A. (1995). Enhancing achievement for language minority students: Classroom, school, and family contexts. *Education and Urban Society, 27*, 441-462.

Geismar, K., & Nicoleau, G. (Eds.). (1993). *Teaching for change: Addressing issues of difference in the college classroom.* Cambridge, MA: Harvard Educational Review.

Gersten, R., & Baker, S. (2000). What we know about effective instructional practices for English language learners. *Exceptional Children, 66,* 454-470.

Gersten, R., Baker, S. K., & Marks, S. U. (1998). *Teaching English-language learners with learning difficulties. Guiding principles and examples from research-based practice.* Reston, VA: Council for Exceptional Children, ERIC Clearinghouse on Disabilities and Gifted Education. (ERIC Document Reproduction Service No. ED 427 448)

Gersten, R., & Jiménez, R. (1998). Modulating instruction for language minority students. In E. J. Kameenui & D. W. Carnine (Eds.), *Effective teaching strategies that accommodate diverse learners* (pp. 161-178). Columbus, OH: Merrill.

Gersten, R., & Woodward, J. (1994). The language minority student and special education: Issues, trends, and paradoxes. *Exceptional Children, 60,* 310-322.

Gibbons, P. (1993). *Learning to learn in a second language.* Portsmouth, NH: Heinemann.

Giroux, H. (1988). *Teachers as intellectuals.* Boston: Bergin & Garvey.

Goldman, S., & Rueda, R. (1988). Developing writing skills in bilingual exceptional children. *Exceptional Children, 54,* 543-551.

Goldstein, B. C. (1995). Critical pedagogy in a bilingual special education classroom. *Journal of Learning Disabilities, 28,* 463-475.

Goldstein, B. C. (1996a). Critical pedagogy in a bilingual special education classroom. In M. Poplin & P. T. Cousin (Eds.), *Alternative views of learning disabilities* (pp. 145-167). Austin, TX: Pro-Ed.

Goldstein, B. C. (1996b). *Discovering voices/creating knowledge: A critical approach to bilingual special education.* Unpublished doctoral dissertation, Claremont Graduate School, Claremont, CA.

González, N., Moll, L. C., Floyd-Tenery, M., Rivera, A., Rendon, P., Gonzáles, R., & Amanti, C. (1993). *Teacher research on funds of knowledge: Learning from households* (Educational Practice Report No. 6). Washington, DC and Santa Cruz, CA: National Center for Research on Cultural Diversity and Second Language Learning

Graden, J. L., Casey, A., & Christenson, S. L. (1985). Implementing a pre-referral intervention system: Part I. The model. *Exceptional Children, 51*, 377-384.

Graves, A. W., Valles, E. C., & Rueda, R. (2000). Variations in interactive writing instruction: A study in four bilingual special education settings. *Learning Disabilities Research, 15*, 1-9.

Graves, D. (1983). *Writing: Teachers and children at work.* Portsmouth, NH: Heinemann.

Greene, G., & Nefsky, P. (1999). Transition for culturally and linguistically diverse youth with disabilities: Closing the gaps. *Multiple Voices for Ethnically Diverse Exceptional Learners, 3*(1), 15-24.

Greenlee, M. (1981). Specifying the needs of a "bilingual" developmentally disabled population: Issues and case studies. *NABE Journal, 6*(1), 55-76.

Grieco, E. M., & Cassidy, R. C. (2001). *Overview of race and Hispanic origin: Census 2000 brief.* Washington, DC: U.S. Bureau of the Census.

Grosjean, F. (1989). Neurolinguists, beware! The bilingual is not two monolinguals in one person. *Brain and Language, 36*, 3-15.

Gudykunst, W. B., & Kim, Y. (1997). *Communicating with strangers: An approach to intercultural communication* (3rd ed.). Boston: McGraw-Hill.

Gudykunst, W. B., & Ting-Toomey, S. (1988). *Culture and interpersonal communication.* Thousand Oaks, CA: Sage.

Gutiérrez, K., & Stone, L. D. (1997). A cultural-historical view of learning and learning disabilities: Participating in a community of learners. *Learning Disabilities Research and Practice, 12*, 123-131.

Gutierrez-Clellen, V. F. (1999). Language choice in intervention with bilingual children. *American Journal of Speech-Language Pathology, 8*, 291-302.

Guy, B., Hasazi, S. B., & Johnson, D. R. (1999). Transition from school to adult life. In M. J. Coutinho & A. C. Repp (Eds.), *Inclusion: The integration of students with disabilities.* Belmont, CA: Wadsworth.

Han, M., Baker, D., & Rodriguez, C. (1997). *A profile of policies and practices for limited English proficient students: Screening methods, program support, and teacher training* [SASS 1993-94, NCES 97-472]. Washington, DC: U.S. Department of Education, National Center for Education Statistics.

Hanson, M. J., Lynch, E. W., & Wayman, K. I. (1990). Honoring the cultural diversity of families when gathering data. *Topics in Early Childhood Special Education, 10*(1), 112-131.

Harry, B. (1992). *Cultural diversity, families, and the special education system: Communication and empowerment.* New York: Teachers College Press.

Harry, B. (1995). African American families. In B. A. Ford, F. E. Obiakor, & J. M. Patton (Eds.), *Effective education of African-American exceptional learners* (pp. 211-233). Austin, TX: Pro-Ed.

Harry, B., Allen, N., & McLaughlin, M. (1995). Communication versus compliance: African-American parents' involvement in special education. *Exceptional Children, 61*, 354-377.

Harry, B., Rueda, R., & Kalyanpur, M. (1999). Cultural reciprocity in sociocultural perspective: Adapting the normalization principle for family collaboration. *Exceptional Children, 66,* 123-136.

Heath, S. B. (1982). What no bedtime story means: Narrative skills at home and school. *Language in Society, 2,* 49-76.

Heath, S. B. (1986). Taking a cross-cultural look at narratives. *Topics in Language Disorders, 7*(1), 84-94.

Heller, K. A., Holtzman, W. H., & Messick, S. (1982). *Placing children in special education: A strategy for equity.* Washington, DC: National Academy Press.

Henderson, A., Abbot, C., & Strang, W. (1993). *Summary of the bilingual education state educational agency program survey of states' limited English proficient persons and available educational services 1991-1992* (Contract No. T292001001, U.S. Department of Education, Office of Bilingual Education and Minority Languages Affairs). Arlington, VA: Development Associates.

Heubert, J. P., & Hauser, R. M. (1999). *High stakes testing for tracking, promotion, and graduation.* Washington, DC: National Academy Press.

Heur, M. B. (1997). Culturally inclusive assessments for children using augmentative and alternative communication (ACC). *Journal of Children's Communication Development, 19*(1), 23-34.

Hilliard, A. (1992, November). *Language, culture, and valid teaching.* Paper presented at the Topical Conference on Culturally and Linguistically Diverse Exceptional Children, Council for Exceptional Children and the Division for Culturally and Linguistically Diverse Exceptional Learners, Minneapolis, MN.

Hodgkinson, H. (1993). American education: The good, the bad, and the task. *Phi Delta Kappan, 74*, 619-623.

Hofstede, G. (1991). *Cultures and organizations: Software of the mind.* New York: McGraw-Hill.

Holtzman, W. H., Jr., & Wilkinson, C. Y. (1991). Assessment of cognitive ability. In E. V. Hamayan & J. S. Damico (Eds.), *Limiting bias in the assessment of bilingual students* (pp. 247-280). Austin, TX: Pro-Ed.

Hopstock, P., & Bucaro, B. (1993). *A review of estimates of LEP student population.* Arlington, VA: Development Associates.

Hung-Hsia, H. (1929). The mentality of the Chinese and Japanese. *Journal of Applied Psychology, 13*, 9-31.

IDEA '97 Final Regulations, Assistance to States for the Education of Children with Disabilities, 34 C.F.R. Part 300 (March 12, 1999). Retrieved January 11, 2001, from http://www.tea.state.tx.us/special.ed

Improving America's Schools Act of 1994, Pub. L. 103-382, Title VII, § 7101 *et seq.*

Individuals With Disabilities Education Act of 1990, Pub. L. 102-119, 20 U.S.C. § 1400 *et seq.*

Individuals With Disabilities Education Act Amendments of 1997, Pub. L. No 94-142, 89 Stat. 773 (as amended), renamed IDEA, Pub. L. No 101-476, 104 Stat. 1143 [codified as amended at 20 U.S.C. § 1400 *et seq*] (1994), amended by the IDEA Amendments of 1997, Pub. L. No.105-17.

Irujo, S. (Ed.). (2000). *Integrating the ESL standards into classroom practice* (Vols. 1-4). Alexandria, VA: Teachers of English to Speakers of Other Languages.

Jensen, A. R. (1976). Construct validity and test bias. *Phi Delta Kappan, 58*, 340-346.

Jensen, A. R. (1980). *Bias in mental testing.* New York: Free Press.

Jensen, A. R., & Inouye, A. R. (1980). Level I and Level II abilities in Asian, White, and Black children. *Intelligence, 4*, 41-49.

Jiménez, R. T., García, G. E., & Pearson, P. D. (1996). The reading strategies of bilingual Latina/o students who are successful English readers: Opportunities and obstacles. *Reading Research Quarterly, 31*(1), 90-112.

Jiménez, R. T., & Gersten, R. (1999). Lesson and dilemmas derived from the literacy instruction of two Latina/o teachers. *American Educational Research Journal, 36*, 265-301.

Jose P. v. Ambach, 557 F. Supp. 11230 (E.D.N.Y. 1983).

Kalyanpur, M., & Harry, B. (1999). *Culture in special education: Building reciprocal family–professional relationships.* Baltimore: Brookes.

Kang, H. W. (1994). Helping second language readers learn from content area text through collaboration and support. *Journal of Reading, 27*, 646-652.

Kayser, H. (1995). Interpreters. In H. Kayser (Ed.), *Bilingual speech–language pathology: An Hispanic focus* (pp. 207-221). San Diego, CA: Singular.

Kindler, A. (2002). *What are the most common language groups for limited English proficient students?* (AskNCBE, No. 5). Washington, DC: National Clearinghouse for Bilingual Education. Retrieved April 8, 2002, from http://www.ncbe.gwu.edu/askncbe/faqs/05toplangs.htm

King-Sears, M. E., Burgess, M., & Lawson, T. L. (1999). Applying curriculum-based assessment in inclusive settings. *Teaching Exceptional Children, 32*(1), 30-38.

Kinsella, K. (1996). Designing group work that supports and enhances diverse classroom work styles. *TESOL Journal, 6*(1), 24-30.

Knapp, M. S., Shields, P. M., & Turnbull, B. J. (1995). Academic challenge in high-poverty classrooms. *Phi Delta Kappan, 16*, 770-776.

Krashen, S. (1982a). Bilingual education and second language acquisition theory. In California State Department of Education, *Schooling and language minority students: A theoretical framework* (pp. 51-79). Los Angeles: Bilingual Education Evaluation, Dissemination, and Assessment Center.

Krashen, S. (1982b). *Principles and practices in second language acquisition.* Oxford, UK: Pergamon.

Krashen, S. (1991). *Bilingual education: A focus on current research* (Occasional Papers in Bilingual Education, No. 3). Washington, DC: National Clearinghouse for Bilingual Education. Retrieved March 26, 2002, from http://www.ncbe.gwu.edu/ncbepubs/focus/focus3.htm

Kroth, R. L., & Edge, D. (1997). *Strategies for communicating with parents and families of exceptional children* (3rd ed.). Denver, CO: Love.

Kuhn, T. (1970). *The structure of scientific revolutions* (2nd ed.). Chicago: University of Chicago Press.

Kushner, M. I., & Ortiz, A. A. (2000). The preparation of early childhood education teachers for English language learners. In *New teachers for a new century: The future of early childhood professional development* (pp. 124-154). Washington, DC: U.S. Department of Education, National Institute on Early Childhood Development and Education.

Langdon, H. (1989). Language disorder or difference? Assessing the language skills of Hispanic students. *Exceptional Children, 56*, 160-167.

Larry P. v. Riles, 343 F. Supp. 1306 (N.D. CA. 1972) affr 502 F.2d 963 (9th Cir. 1974); 495 F. Supp. 926 (N.D. CA. 1979).

Lau v. Nichols, 414 U.S. 563 (1974).

Leinhardt, G. (1992). What research on learning tells us about teaching. *Educational Leadership, 49*(7), 20-25.

Leung, B. P. (1996). Quality assessment practices in a diverse society. *Teaching Exceptional Children, 28*(3), 42-45.

Leverett, R. G., & Diefendorf, A. O. (1992, Summer). Students with language deficiencies. *Teaching Exceptional Children, 24*(4), 30-34.

Lipsky, D. K., & Gartner, A. (1999). Inclusive education: A requirement of a democratic society. In H. Daniels & P. Garner (Eds.), *World yearbook of education 1999: Inclusive education* (pp. 12-23). London: Kogan Page.

López, E. C. (1995). Best practices in working with bilingual children. In A. Thomas & J. Grimes (Eds.), *Best practices in school psychology III* (pp. 1111-1121). Washington, DC: National Association of School Psychologists.

López-Reyna, N. (1996). The importance of meaningful contexts in bilingual special education: Moving to whole language. *Learning Disabilities Research and Practice, 11*, 120-131.

Lubeck, S. (1994). The politics of developmentally appropriate practice: Exploring issues of culture, class, and curriculum. In B. L. Mallory & R. S. New (Eds.), *Diversity and developmentally appropriate practices: Challenges for early childhood education* (pp. 17-43). New York: Columbia University, Teachers College.

Luh, C. W., & Wy, T. M. (1931). A comparative study of the intelligence of Chinese children on the Pintner performance and the Binet tests. *Journal of Social Psychology, 2*, 402-408.

Lynch, E. W., & Hanson, M. J. (Eds.). (1998). *Developing cross-cultural competence: A guide for working with young children and their families* (2nd ed.). Baltimore: Paul H. Brookes.

Lynch, E. W., & Stein, R. (1987). Parent participation by ethnicity: A comparison of Hispanic, Black, and Anglo families. *Exceptional Children, 54*, 105-111.

Lyons, J. L. (1992). *Legal responsibilities of education agencies serving national origin language minority children.* Chevy Chase, MD: Mid-Atlantic Equity Center.

Macías, R. (1998). *Summary report of the survey of the states' limited English proficient students and available educational programs and services: 1996-1997.* Washington, DC: National Clearinghouse for Bilingual Education. Retrieved May 20, 2002, from http://www.ncbe.gwu.edu/ncbepubs/seareports/96-97/part1.htm

Madden, N. A., Slavin, R. E., Karweit, N. L., Dolan, L., & Wasik, B. A. (1991). Success for All. *Phi Delta Kappan, 72*, 593-599.

Maheady, L., Towne, R., Algozzine, B., Mercer, J., & Ysseldyke, J. E. (1983). Minority overrepresentation: A case for alternative practices prior to referral. *Learning Disability Quarterly, 6*, 448-456.

Manuel, H. T. (1935). *Spanish and English editions of the Stanford-Binet in relation to the abilities of Mexican children* (University of Texas Bulletin No. 3532). Austin: University of Texas.

Mattes, L. J., & Omark, D. R. (1984). *Speech and language assessment for the bilingual handicapped.* San Diego, CA: College Hill Press.

McGoldrick, M., Pearce, J., & Giordano, J. (1982). *Ethnicity and family therapy.* New York: Guilford.

McGroarty, M. (1989). The benefits of cooperative learning arrangements in second language instruction. *National Association for Bilingual Education Journal, 13*(2), 127-143.

McLaren, P. (1994). *Life in schools.* New York: Longman.

McLaughlin, M. J., Artiles, A. J., & Pullin, D. (2001). Challenges for the transformation of special education in the 21st century: Rethinking culture in school reform. *Journal of Special Education Leadership, 14,* 51-62.

McLaughlin, M. J., Nolet, V., Rhim, L. M., & Henderson, K. (1999). Integrating standards: Including all students. *Teaching Exceptional Children, 31*(3), 66-71.

Mehan, H., Hartweck, H., & Meihls, J. L. (1986). *Handicapping the handicapped.* Palo Alto, CA: Stanford University Press.

Méndez Pérez, A. (1998). *Mexican-American mothers' perceptions and beliefs about language acquisition among toddlers with language disabilities.* Unpublished doctoral dissertation, University of Texas at Austin.

Mercer, J. R. (1973). *Labeling the mentally retarded.* Berkeley: University of California Press.

Mercer, J. R. (1992). The impact of changing paradigms of disability on mental retardation in the year 2000. In L. Rowitz (Ed.), *Mental retardation in the year 2000* (pp. 15-38). New York: Springer-Verlag.

Moll, L. (Ed.). (1990). *Vygotsky and education: Instructional implications and applications of sociocultural psychology.* New York: Cambridge University Press.

Moll, L. (1992). Bilingual classroom studies and community analysis: Some recent trends. *Educational Researcher, 21*(2), 20-24.

Moll, L., Amanti, C. A., Neff, D., & González, N. (1992). Funds of knowledge for teaching: Using a qualitative approach to connect homes and classrooms. *Theory Into Practice, 31*(2), 132-141.

Muñoz-Sandoval, A. F., Cummins, J., Alvarado, C. G., & Rueff, M. (1998). *Bilingual Verbal Ability Tests: Comprehensive manual.* Itasca, IL: Riverside.

National Center for Educational Statistics. (1999). *Digest of education statistics.* Washington, DC: U.S. Department of Education, Office of Educational Research and Improvement.

National Center for Educational Statistics. (2000). *The condition of education.* Washington, DC: U.S. Department of Education, Office of Educational Research and Improvement.

National Clearinghouse for Bilingual Education. (1995, Fall). The changing face of America's schools. F*orum, 8*(4). Retrieved October 23, 2001, from http://www.ncbe.gwu.edu/ncbepubs/forum/1804.htm

National Clearinghouse for Bilingual Education. (1996). *Why is it important to maintain the native language?* (AskNCBE, No. 12). Washington, DC: Author. Retrieved October 23, 2001, from http://www.ncbe.gwu.edu/askncbe/faqs/12native.htm

National Education Goals Panel. (1995). *Data volume for the National Education Goals report. Vol. 1: National data.* Washington, DC: U.S. Government Printing Office.

National Governors' Association. (1987). *Bringing down the barriers.* Washington, DC: Author.

National Institute of Human Development. (1998). *Why children succeed or fail at reading: Research from the National Institute of Child, Health, and Human Development (NICHD) extramural program in learning disabilities.* Rockville, MD: National Institute of Child, Health, and Human Development, Public Information and Communications Branch.

Oakes, J. (1986). *Keeping track: How schools structure inequality.* New Haven, CT: Yale University Press.

Office of Civil Rights. (1997). *1994 elementary and secondary school civil rights compliance report projected values for the nation (revised).* Washington, DC: U.S. Department of Education, Office of Civil Rights.

Ogbu, J. (1994). From cultural differences to differences in cultural frames of reference. In P. M. Greenfield & R. R. Cocking (Eds.), *Cross-cultural roots of minority child development* (pp. 365-392). Hillsdale, NJ: Lawrence Erlbaum.

Olson, J. F., & Goldstein, A. A. (1997). *The inclusion of students with disabilities and limited English proficiency in large-scale assessments: A summary of a recent progress.* Washington, DC: U.S. Department of Education.

Ortiz, A. A. (1984). Choosing the language of instruction for exceptional bilingual children. *Teaching Exceptional Children, 16*(3), 208-212.

Ortiz, A. A. (1990, Fall). Using school-based problem-solving teams for prereferral intervention. *Bilingual Special Education Newsletter, 10*(1), 3-5.

Ortiz, A. A. (1991). *Aim for the BESt: Assessment and intervention model for the bilingual exceptional student. A handbook for teachers and planners from the Innovative Approaches Research Project.* Austin, TX and Arlington, VA: University of Texas at Austin Department of Special Education and Development Associates.

Ortiz, A. A. (1997). Learning disabilities occurring concomitantly with linguistic differences. *Journal of Learning Disabilities, 30*, 321-332.

Ortiz, A. A. (2000). Including students with special needs in standards-based reform: Issues associated with the alignment of standards, curriculum, and instruction. In *Mid-continent Research for Education and Learning: Including special needs students in standards-based reform* (pp. 41-64). Aurora, CO: McREL.

Ortiz, A. A., & García, S. B. (1990). Using language assessment data for language and instructional planning for exceptional bilingual students. In A. Carrasquillo & R. Baecher (Eds.), *Teaching the bilingual special education student* (pp. 24-47). Norwood, NJ: Ablex.

Ortiz, A. A., García, S. B., Holtzman, Jr., W. H., Polyzoi, E., Snell, W. E., Jr., Wilkinson, C. Y., & Willig, A. C. (1985). *Characteristics of limited English proficient Hispanic students in programs of the learning disabled: Implications for policy, practice, and research.* Austin: University of Texas, Handicapped Minority Research Institute on Language Proficiency.

Ortiz, A. A., García, S. B., Wheeler, D., & Maldonado-Colón, E. (1986). *Characteristics of limited English proficient students served in programs for the speech and language handicapped: Implications for policy, practice, and research.* Austin: University of Texas, Handicapped Minority Research Institute on Language Proficiency.

Ortiz, A. A., & Graves, A. (2001). English language learners with literacy-related disabilities. *International Dyslexia Association Commemorative Booklet* (pp. 31-35). Baltimore: International Dyslexia Association.

Ortiz, A. A., & Kushner, M. I. (1997). Bilingualism and the possible impact on academic performance. *Child and Adolescent Psychiatric Clinics of North America, 6,* 657-679.

Ortiz, A. A., & Wilkinson, C. Y. (1991). Assessment and Intervention Model for the Bilingual Exceptional Student (AIM for the BEST). *Teacher Education and Special Education, 14*(1), 35-42.

Ortiz, A. A., & Yates, J. R. (1983). Incidence of exceptionality among Hispanics: Implications for manpower planning. *National Association for Bilingual Education Journal, 7*(3), 41-53.

Ortiz, A. A., & Yates, J. R. (2001). A framework for serving English language learners with disabilities. *Journal of Special Education Leadership, 14*(2), 72-80.

Palincsar, A. M., & Brown, A. L. (1984). Reciprocal teaching of comprehension-fostering and comprehension monitoring activities. *Cognition and Instruction, 1*(2), 117-175.

Palincsar, A. M., & Brown, A. L. (1989). Classroom dialogues to promote self-regulated comprehension. *Advances in Research on Teaching, 1,* 35-71.

Parette, H. P., & Petch-Hogan, B. (2000). Approaching families: Facilitating culturally/linguistically diverse family involvement. *Teaching Exceptional Children, 33*(2), 4-11.

Payan, R. (1984). Language assessment for bilingual exceptional children. In L. M. Baca & H. T. Cervantes (Eds.), *The bilingual special education interface* (pp. 15-137). St Louis, MO: Times Mirror/Mosby.

Pederson, P. B. (1981). Alternative futures for cross-cultural counseling and psychotherapy. In A. J. Marsella & P. B. Pedersen (Eds.), *Cross-cultural counseling and psychotherapy* (pp. 312-337). New York: Pergamon.

Pellegrino, J. W., Jones, L. R., & Mitchell, K. J. (Eds.). (1999). *Grading the nation's report card: Evaluating NAEP and transforming the assessment of educational progress.* Washington, DC: National Academy Press.

Peregoy, S. F., & Boyle, O. F. (1997). *Reading, writing, & learning in ESL: A resource book for K–12 teachers* (2nd ed.). White Plains, NY: Longman.

Polloway, E. A., Patton, J. R., & Serna, L. (2001). *Strategies for teaching learners with special needs* (7th ed.). Upper Saddle River, NJ: Merrill Prentice Hall.

Poplin, M. (1988). The reductionist fallacy in learning disabilities: Replicating the past by reducing the present. *Journal of Learning Disabilities, 21*, 389-400.

Reyes, E. I., & Bos, C. S. (1996). Interactive semantic mapping and charting: Enhancing content area learning for language minority students. In R. M. Gersten & R. T. Jiménez (Eds.), *Promoting learning for culturally and linguistically diverse students* (pp. 133-150). Belmont, CA: Wadsworth.

Rice, L. S. (1995). *Factors related to disproportionate representation of Hispanics in programs for students with learning disabilities.* Unpublished doctoral dissertation, University of Texas at Austin.

Rice, L. S., & Ortiz, A. A. (1994). Second language difference or learning disabilities? *LD Forum, 19*(2), 11-13.

Robertson, P., Kushner, M. I., Starks, J., & Drescher, C. (1994). An update of participation rates of culturally and linguistically diverse students in special education: The need for a research and policy agenda. *The Bilingual Special Education Perspective, 14*(1), 3-9.

Rogoff, B. (1991). Social interaction as apprenticeship in thinking: Guidance and participation in spatial planning. In L. B. Resnick, J. M. Levine, and S. Teasley (Eds.), *Perspectives on socially shared cognition* (pp. 349-364). Washington, DC: American Psychological Association.

Romero de Thompson, S. (1996). *Hondurans in the United States: Their perceptions and beliefs about mental health, mental illness, and service utilization.* Unpublished doctoral dissertation, University of Texas at Austin.

Roseberry-McKibbin, C. (1995). *Multicultural students with special language needs: Practical strategies for assessment and intervention.* Oceanside, CA: Academic Communication Associates.

Rueda, R. (1984). Cognitive development and learning in mildly handicapped bilingual children. In P. Chinn (Ed.), *Education of culturally and linguistically different exceptional children.* Reston, VA: Council for Exceptional Children, ERIC Clearinghouse on Handicapped and Gifted Children. (ERIC Document Reproduction Service No. ED 256 106)

Rueda, R. (1989). Defining mild disabilities with language minority students. *Exceptional Children, 56*(2), 121-128.

Rueda, R. (1990). An analysis of special education as a response to the diminished academic achievement of Chicano Students. In R. Valencia (Ed.), *Chicano school failure and success: Research and policy agendas for the 1990s* (pp. 253-270). New York: Falmer.

Rueda, R. (1993). *Theoretical perspectives on LH and assessment 1950–present.* Paper presented at the Fiesta Educativa Conference, University of Southern California, Los Angeles.

Rueda, R., Artiles, A. J., Salazar, J., & Higareda, I. (in press). An analysis of special education as a response to the diminished academic achievement of Chicano students: An update. In R. Valencia (Ed.), *Chicano school failure and success: Research and policy agendas* (2nd ed.). London: Falmer.

Rueda, R., Figueroa, R., Mercado, P., & Cardoza, D. (1984). *Performance of Hispanic educable mentally retarded learning disabled and nonclassified students on the WISC-RM, SOMPA and S-KABC.* Los Alamitos, CA: Southwest Regional Laboratory.

Rueda, R., & Goldman, S. (1988). Developing writing skills in bilingual exceptional children. *Exceptional Children, 54*, 543-551.

Rueda, R., & Mehan, H. (1986). Metacognition and passing: Strategic interaction in the lives of students with learning disabilities. *Anthropology and Education Quarterly, 17*, 145-165.

Ruiz, N. T. (1989). An optimal learning environment for Rosemary. *Exceptional Children, 56*, 130-144.

Ruiz, N. T. (1995a). The social construction of ability and disability: I. Profile types of Latino children identified as language learning disabled. *Journal of Learning Disabilities, 28*, 476-490.

Ruiz, N. T. (1995b). The social construction of ability and disability: II. Optimal and at-risk lessons in a bilingual special education classroom. *Journal of Learning Disabilities, 28*, 491-502.

Ruiz, N. T. (1999). Effective literacy instruction for Latino students receiving special education services: A review of classroom research. In T. Fletcher & C. Bos (Eds.), *U.S./Mexican perspectives on disabilities.* Tempe, AZ: Bilingual Review Press.

Ruiz, N. T., & Enguidanos, T. (1997). Authenticity and advocacy in assessment: Bilingual students in special education. *Primary Voices –6, 5*(3), 35-46.

Ruiz, N. T., & Figueroa, R. A. (1995). Learning-handicapped classroom with Latino students: The optimal learning environment (OLE) project. *Education and Urban Society, 27,* 463-483.

Ruiz, N. T., García, E., & Figueroa, R. A. (1996). *The OLE curriculum guide: Creating optimal learning environments for students from diverse backgrounds in special and general education.* Sacramento: California Department of Education.

Ruiz, N. T., Rueda, R., Figueroa, R. A., & Boothroyd, M. (1995). Bilingual special education teachers' shifting paradigms: Complex responses to educational reform. *Journal of Learning Disabilities, 28,* 622-635.

Salend, S. J. (1998). Using portfolios to assess student performance. *Teaching Exceptional Children, 31*(2), 36-43.

Sanchez, S. (1999). Learning from the stories of culturally and linguistically diverse families and communities: A sociohistorical lens. *Remedial and Special Education, 20,* 351-359.

Sanchez-Boyce, M. (2000). *The use of interpreters in special education assessments.* Unpublished doctoral disserstation, University of California at Davis.

Santos, R. M., Fowler, S. A., Corso, R. M., & Bruns, D. A. (2000). Acceptance, acknowledgement, and adaptability. Selecting culturally and linguistically appropriate early childhood materials. *Teaching Exceptional Children, 32*(3), 14-22.

Scarcella, R. (1990). *Teaching language minority students in the multicultural classroom.* Englewood Cliffs, NJ: Prentice Hall.

Schön, D. A. (1983). *The reflective practitioner.* San Francisco: Jossey-Bass.

Schumaker, J. D., Nolan, S. M., & Deshler, D. D. (1985). *The error monitoring strategy.* Lawrence: University of Kansas, Center for Research on Learning.

Segura-Mora, A. (1998). Critical pedagogy and the education of young children. In J. Frederickson (Series Ed.) and A. Darder (Vol. Ed.), *Reclaiming our voices: Emancipatory narratives on critical literacy, praxis, and pedagogy; Teaching as an act of love: Reflections on Paulo Freire and his contributions to our lives and our work* (pp. 62-65). Los Angeles: California Association for Bilingual Education.

Shakrani, S. (1999). *Standardized achievement tests and English language learners: Validity and fairness.* Los Angeles: University of California, National Center for Research on Evaluation, Standards, and Student Testing (CRESST).

Shinn, M. R., & Tindal, G. A. (1988). Using student performance data in academics: A pragmatic and defensible approach to non-discriminatory assessment. In R. G. Jones (Ed.), *Psychoeducational assessment of minority group children: A casebook* (pp. 383-407). Berkeley, CA: Cobb & Henry.

Singh, S. (1986). Adolescent pregnancy in the United States: Interstate analysis. *Family Planning Perspectives, 18,* 210-220.

Skrtic, T. M. (1988). The crisis in special education knowledge. In E. L. Meyen & T. M. Skrtic (Eds.), *Exceptional children and youth* (3rd ed., pp. 415-447). Denver, CO: Love.

Skrtic, T. M. (1991). The special education paradox: Equity as the way to excellence. *Harvard Educational Review, 61,* 148-186.

Skrtic, T. M. (Ed.). (1995). *Disability and democracy.* New York: Teachers College Press.

Slavin, R. E., & Madden, N. A. (1989). What works for students at risk: A research synthesis. *Educational Leadership, 46*(5), 4-13.

Sleeter, C. E. (1986). Learning disabilities: The social construction of a special education category. *Exceptional Children, 39,* 651-652.

Smith, D. D. (2001). *Introduction to special education: Teaching in an age of opportunity* (4th ed.). Boston: Allyn and Bacon.

Smith, M. S., Fuhrman, S. H., & O'Day, J. (1994). In R. F. Elmore & S. H. Fuhrman (Eds.), *The governance of curriculum: 1994 Yearbook of the Association for Supervision and Curriculum Development* (pp. 12-29). Alexandria, VA: ASCD.

Snow, C., Burns, M. S., & Griffin, P. (Eds). (1998). *Preventing reading difficulties in young children.* Washington, DC: National Academy Press.

Sontag, J. C., & Schacht, R. (1994). An ethnic comparison of parent participation and information needs in early intervention. *Exceptional Children, 60,* 422-433.

Spener, D. (1992). *The Freirean approach to adult literacy education.* Washington, DC: National Clearinghouse for ESL Literacy Education. Retrieved April 7, 2002, from http://www.cal.org/ncle/digests/FreireQA.htm

Spindler, G., & Spindler, L. (Eds.). (1994). *Pathways to cultural awareness: Cultural therapy with teachers and students.* Thousand Oaks, CA: Corwin.

Stedman, L. C. (1987). It's time we changed the effective schools formula. *Phi Delta Kappan, 69,* 215-224.

Stewner-Manzanares, G. (1988). *The Bilingual Education Act: Twenty years later* (New Focus, No. 6). Washington, DC: National Clearinghouse for Bilingual Education. Retrieved May 20, 2002, from http://www.ncbe.gwu.edu/ncbepubs/classics/focus/06bea.htm

Swanson, H. L. (1999). Reading research for students with LD: A meta-analysis of intervention outcomes. *Journal of Learning Disabilities, 32*, 504-532.

Swanson, H. L. (2000). What instruction works for students with learning disabilities? Summarizing the results from a meta-analysis of intervention studies. In R. M. Gersten, E. P. Schiller, & S. Vaughn (Eds.), *Issues in research in special education* (pp. 1-30). Mahwah, NJ: Lawrence Erlbaum Associates.

Swicegood, P. (1994). Portfolio-based assessment practices: The uses of portfolio assessment for students with behavioral disorders or learning disabilities. *Intervention in School and Clinic, 30*(1), 6-15.

Taylor, S. V. (2000). Multicultural is who we are. *Teaching Exceptional Children, 32*(3), 24-29.

Teachers of English to Speakers of Other Languages. (1996). *Promising futures: ESL standards for pre-K–12 students* (TESOL Professional Papers No. 1). Alexandria, VA: Author.

Teachers of English to Speakers of Other Languages. (1997). *The ESL standards for pre-K–12 students.* Alexandria, VA: Author.

Tharp, R. (1997). *From at-risk to excellence: Research, theory, and principles for practice.* Santa Cruz, CA: Center for Research on Education, Diversity & Excellence.

Tharp, R. G., Dalton, S., & Yamauchi, L. A. (1994). Principles for culturally compatible Native American education. *Journal of Navajo Education, 11(3)*, 21-27.

Tharp, R. G., Estrada, P., Dalton, S. S., & Yamauchi, L. A. (2000). *Teaching transformed: Achieving excellence, fairness, inclusion, and harmony.* Boulder, CO: Westview.

Tharp, R. G., & Gallimore, R. (1988). *Rousing minds to life: Teaching, learning, and schooling in social context.* New York: Cambridge University Press.

Thomas, W. P., & Collier, V. (1997, December). *School effectiveness for language minority students* (Resource Collection Series, No. 9). Washington, DC: National Clearinghouse for Bilingual Education. Retrieved April 20, 2002, http://www.ncbe.gwu.edu/ncbepubs/resource/effectiveness/index.htm

Thousand, J., Diaz-Greenberg, R., Nevin, A., Cardelle-Elawar, M., Beckett, E. C., & Reese, R. (1999). Perspectives on a Freirean dialectic to promote inclusive education. *Remedial and Special Education, 20*(6), 323-326.

Trueba, H. T. (1987). Cultural differences or learning handicaps? Towards an understanding of adjustment processes. In *Proceedings of the University of California Linguistic Minority Research Project Conference: Vol. III. Schooling language minority youth* (pp. 45-79). Los Angeles, CA: University of California.

Trumbull, E., Rothstein-Fisch, C., Greenfield, P. M., & Quiroz, B. (2001). *Bridging cultures between home and school: A guide for teachers.* Mahwah, NJ: Lawrence Erlbaum.

Tucker, J. A. (1985). Curriculum-based assessment: An introduction. *Exceptional Children, 52*(3), 199-204.

Turnbull, A. P., Pereira, L., & Blue-Banning, M. (2000). Teachers as friendship facilitators: *Respeto* and *personalismo. Teaching Exceptional Children, 32*(5), 66-70.

United Cerebral Palsy (UCP) of New York v. Board of Education of the City of New York, 79 C. 560 (E.D.N.Y. 1979).

U.S. Census Bureau. (n.d.). *Census 2000 supplementary survey: Profile of selected social characteristics.* Retrieved April 22, 2002, from http://factfinder.census.gov/home/en/c2ss.html

U.S. Commission on Civil Rights. (1997). *Equal educational opportunity and nondiscrimination for students with disabilities: Federal enforcement of Section 504. Equal educational opportunity project series, Volume II.* Washington, DC: Author.

U.S. Department of Education. (1999). *21st report to Congress on the implementation of the IDEA act.* Washington, DC: Author.

U.S. Department of Education. (2000). *Nondiscrimination in high-stake testing: A resource guide.* Washington, DC: U.S. Department of Education, Office for Civil Rights.

U.S. Department of State, Bureau of Population, Refugees, and Migration. (2002). *U.S. refugee admissions and resettlement program.* Retrieved April 22, 2002, from http://www.usinfo.state.gov/topical/global/refugees/adover.htm

Valdés, G., & Figueroa, R. A. (1994). *Bilingualism and testing: A special case of bias.* Norwood, NJ: Ablex.

Vandegrift, J. A., & Greene, A. L. (1992). Rethinking parent involvement. *Educational Leadership, 50*(1), 57-59.

Viera, D. (1986). Remediating reading problems in a Hispanic learning disabled child from a psycholinguistic perspective: A case study. In A. C. Willig & H. F. Greenberg (Eds.), *Bilingualism and learning disabilities* (pp. 81-92). New York: American Library.

Vocational Rehabilitation Act of 1973. Pub. L. No. 93-112, 19 U.S.C. § 504.

Vygotsky, L. S. (1978). *Mind in society: The development of higher psychological processes* (M. Cole, V. John-Steiner, S. Scribner, & E. Souberman, Eds. and Trans.). Cambridge, MA: Harvard University Press.

Walberg, H. J., Bakalis, M. J., Bast, J. L., & Baer, S. (1989). Reconstructing the nation's worst schools. *Phi Delta Kappan, 70*, 802-805.

Wang, M. C., Reynolds, M. C., & Walberg, H. J. (1995). Serving students at the margins. *Educational Leadership, 52*(4), 12-17.

Wein, C. A. (1995). *Developmentally appropriate practice in "real life."* New York: Teachers College Press.

Weisner, T. S., Gallimore, T., & Jordan. C. (1988). Unpacking cultural effects on classroom learning: Native Hawaiian peer assistance and child-generated activity. *Anthropology & Education Quarterly, 19*, 327-351.

Wells, G. H. (1998, February). *Talk, text, and inquiry: Schooling as a semiotic apprenticeship.* Paper presented at the Language Reading and Culture Colloquium, University of Arizona, Tempe, AZ.

Wertheimer, C., & Honigsfeld, A. (2000). Preparing ESL students to meet the new standards. *TESOL Journal, 9*(1), 23-28.

Wertsch, J. V. (1991). *Voices of the mind: A sociocultural approach to mediated action.* Cambridge, MA: Harvard University Press.

Wilkinson, C. Y., & Ortiz, A. A. (1986). *Characteristics of limited English proficient and English proficient learning disabled Hispanic students at initial assessment and at reevaluation.* Austin: University of Texas, Department of Special Education, Handicapped Minority Research Institute on Language Proficiency. (ERIC Document Reproduction Service No. ED 283 314)

Willig, A. C., & Swedo, J. (1987, April). *Improving teaching strategies for exceptional Hispanic limited English proficient students: An exploratory study of task engagement and teaching strategies.* Paper presented at the meeting of the American Educational Research Association, Washington, DC.

Willig, A. C., Swedo, J. J., & Ortiz, A. A. (1987). *Characteristics of teaching strategies which result in high task engagement for exceptional limited English proficient students.* Austin: University of Texas at Austin, Handicapped Minority Research Institute on Language Proficiency.

Winzer, M. A., & Mazurek, K. (1998). *Special education in multicultural contexts.* Upper Saddle River, NJ: Merrill.

Wood, D., Bruner, J. S., & Ross, G. (1976). The role of tutoring in problem solving. *Journal of Child Psychology and Psychiatry, 17,* 98-100.

Woodcock, R. W., & Johnson, M. B. C. (1989). *Woodcock-Johnson Psychoeducational Battery-Revised.* Itasca, IL: Riverside.

Woodcock, R. W., & Muñoz-Sandoval, A. F. (1996). *Batería Woodcock-Muñoz-Revisida.* Itasca, IL: Riverside.

Wyatt, J. D. (1978-1979). Native involvement in curriculum development: The native teacher as cultural broker. *Interchange, 9,* 17-28.

Yates, J. R., & Ortiz, A. A. (1991). Professional development needs of teachers who serve exceptional language minorities in today's schools. *Teacher Education and Special Education, 14*(1), 11-18.

Yates, J. R., & Ortiz, A. A. (1998a). Developing individualized education programs for exceptional language minority students. In L. Baca & H. Cervantes (Eds.), *The bilingual special education interface* (pp. 188-213). Upper Saddle River, NJ: Prentice Hall.

Yates, J. R., & Ortiz, A. A. (1998b). Issues of culture and diversity affecting educators with disabilities: A change in demography is reshaping America. In R. J. Anderson, C. E. Keller, & J. M. Karp (Eds.), *Enhancing diversity: Educators with disabilities in the education enterprise* (pp. 21-37). Washington, DC: Gallaudet University Press.

Zehler, A. M. (1994). *Working with English language learners: Strategies for elementary and middle school teachers* (Program Information Guide, No. 19). Washington, DC: National Clearinghouse for Bilingual Education. Retrieved May 20, 2002, from *http://www.ncbe. gwu.edu/ncbepubs/pigs/pig19.htm*

About the Contributors

Alfredo J. Artiles

Alfredo J. Artiles (aj.artiles@vanderbilt.edu) is an associate professor at Peabody College at Vanderbilt University. He has expertise in teacher learning for student diversity and in multiculturalism in special education. His research interests include minority representation in special education, teacher learning in multicultural contexts, and comparative studies of equity issues in special education.

Leonard M. Baca

Leonard Baca (Leonard.Baca@Colorado.edu) is a professor of education at the University of Colorado at Boulder, specializing in bilingual education and bilingual special education. He is the founder and director of the BUENO Center for Multicultural Education. Nationally recognized for his research on English language learners with disabilities and for his contributions to the development of the bilingual special education field, Dr. Baca is the coauthor of one of the best-known texts in the field, *The Bilingual Special Education Interface.*

Candace S. Bos

Candace S. Bos was a professor of special education at the University of Texas at Austin from 1999 until her death in 2001. Before joining the University of Texas faculty, she taught at the University of Arizona. Dr. Bos was nationally recognized for her teaching, her research in the field of special education, and her work related to learning disabilities. She was a fellow of the International Academy for Research in Learning Disabilities and a recipient of the Samuel A. Kirk Outstanding Teaching Award. She authored numerous books and more than 100 scholarly articles.

Nancy Cloud

Nancy Cloud (Ncloud@ric.edu) is an associate professor in the Department of Special Education in the Feinstein School of Education and Human Development at Rhode Island College. A member of the 2000-2003 TESOL Board of Directors, she is a specialist in multicultural special education. Her interests include the preparation of teachers for increasingly diverse schools and the design and delivery of curricula and instruction that address the needs of learners with diverse cultural backgrounds and ability levels.

Richard A. Figueroa

Richard A. Figueroa (rafigueroa@ucdavis.edu) is a professor of education at the University of California, Davis. He served as the commissioner of California's Advisory Commission on Special Education. His research interests include the psychoeducational assessment of bilingual students, bilingual special education, and the educational needs of migrant students. He is involved in judicial initiatives to correct the overrepresentation of minority children in special education programs. His most recent publication is *Testing Hispanic Students in the United States: Technical and Policy Issues*, a report to the President's Advisory Commission on Educational Excellence for Hispanic Americans

Todd V. Fletcher

Todd V. Fletcher (toddf@u.arizona.edu) is an associate professor in the Department of Special Education, Rehabilitation, and School Psychology in the College of Education at the University of Arizona. A graduate of the University of the Americas in Puebla, Mexico, he is a leading authority on special education in Mexico. His research interests include English language acquisition, assessment and instructional practices for students from culturally diverse backgrounds, and special education reform in Latin America.

Shernaz B. García

Shernaz B. García (sbgarcia@mail.utexas.edu) is an associate professor in the Department of Special Education at the University of Texas at Austin. Her teaching and research interests include intercultural communication in the classroom, effective programs for language minority students at educational risk, the disproportionate representation of students from culturally diverse backgrounds in special education, bilingual and multicultural special education, and teacher education.

Barbara S. C. Goldstein

Barbara S. C. Goldstein (goldsteb@aol.com) is an associate professor in the Department of School Psychology and Counseling at Azusa Pacific University. Formerly she served as the director of special education at California Lutheran University. Her research interests include the application of critical pedagogy to special education classes, the use of children's literature in the development of critical literacy, educational consultant practices in bicultural communities, and the creation of Spanish-speaking parent networks for advocacy in special education.

Alba A. Ortiz

Alba A. Ortiz (alba.ortiz@mail.utexas.edu) is a professor in the Department of Special Education at the College of Education in the University of Texas at Austin, where she is also the director of the Office of Bilingual Education. She is the holder of the President's Chair for Education Academic Excellence. Her research and teaching interests include early intervention strategies for English language learners experiencing academic difficulties, the assessment of oral language skills, and special education service delivery for English language learners with language and learning disabilities.

Lorri Johnson Santamaría

Lorri Johnson Santamaría (lsantama@csusm.edu; drsanta@cox.net) is an assistant professor of Multicultural/Multilingual Education at California State University San Marcos. As a member of the 1999-2001 Council of Chief State School Officers (CCSSO) Special Education Standards Committee of the Interstate New Teacher Assessment and Support Consortium (INTASC), she helped to draft the curriculum standards for students with disabilities. She specializes in the professional development of teachers of mainstreamed students who come from culturally diverse backgrounds and have learning disabilities. She is also interested in instruction that helps these students succeed in the general education class.

James R. Yates

James R. Yates (yates@mail.utexas.edu) is the John L. and Elizabeth G. Hill Centennial Professor in Education at the University of Texas at Austin. He has a joint appointment in the Departments of Educational Administration and Special Education, where his teaching focuses on the preparation of educational leaders with a particular emphasis on special education administration. His research interests include demography, the disproportionate representation of multicultural populations in special education, and techniques for forecasting and responding to changes in education.